A STUDENT'S GUIDE TO COLLEGE TRANSITION

April Herring, Ed.D.

❀ cognella® | ACADEMIC PUBLISHING

Bassim Hamadeh, CEO and Publisher
Kassie Graves, Acquisitions Editor
Berenice Quirino, Associate Production Editor
Miguel Macias, Senior Graphic Designer
Alexa Lucido, Licensing Associate
Don Kesner, Interior Designer
Natalie Piccotti, Senior Marketing Manager
Kassie Graves, Director of Acquisitions and Sales
Jamie Giganti, Senior Managing Editor

Cover image copyright © 2015 iStockphoto LP/sturti.

Printed in the United States of America

ISBN: 978-1-5165-1656-8 (pbk)

cognella® | ACADEMIC PUBLISHING

A STUDENT'S GUIDE TO COLLEGE TRANSITION

THE COGNELLA SERIES ON STUDENT SUCCESS

S tudent success isn't always measured in straight As.

Many students arrive at college believing that if they study hard and earn top grades, their higher education experience will be a success. Few recognize that some of their greatest learning opportunities will take place outside the classroom. Learning how to manage stress, navigate new relationships, or put together a budget can be just as important as acing a pop quiz.

The Cognella Series on Student Success is a collection of books designed to help students develop the essential life and learning skills needed to support a happy, healthy, and productive higher education experience. Featuring topics suggested by students and books written by experts, the series offers research-based, yet practical advice to help any student navigate new challenges and succeed throughout their college experience.

Series Editor: Richard Parsons, Ph.D.

Professor of Counselor Education, West Chester University

Other titles available in the series:

- *A Student's Guide to Stress Management*

- *A Student's Guide to a Meaningful Career*

- *A Student's Guide to Self-Care*

- *A Student's Guide to Money Matters*

- *A Student's Guide to Communication and Self-Presentation*

- *A Student's Guide to Exercise for Improving Health*

ABOUT THE AUTHOR

Want to know a secret? There's more to college than studying and going to class!

A Student's Guide to College Transitions highlights the myriad opportunities that are available to you outside the classroom and why it's in your best interest to get out there and participate in them. The guide helps you understand how cultivating new experiences and developing diverse skill sets can not only enrich your overall college experience, but make you a more attractive candidate for future academic programs and employment opportunities.

Growth and learning opportunities aren't confined to a course or classroom. This guide will show you how to get more out of your college experience by leveraging extra-curricular activities and experiences.

A Student's Guide to College Transition is part of the Cognella Series on Student Success, a collection of books designed to help students develop the essential life and learning skills needed to support a happy, healthy, and productive higher education experience.

Dr. April Herring has worked and taught at public, private, and community colleges in her 25 year career in higher education. She has lived in residence halls with students, taught students in the classroom, served as an academic advisor, planned orientation, advised student clubs, and done many other things with and for college students. It was through these activities that she figured out who she is and what she wanted to do with her life. In her 25 years of experience in higher education she continues to see students grow and learn outside of the class in ways that are profound and meaningful.

CONTENTS

The Cognella Series on Student Success v

About the Author vii

Editor's Preface xi

Chapter 1 There's More to College than Classes 1

Chapter 2 Should I Work and If So, Where? 13

Chapter 3 Work Experience Opportunities 21

Chapter 4 Life Outside the United States 31

Chapter 5 Community Service 43

Chapter 6 Clubs and Organizations 53

Chapter 7 Playing a Sport in College 75

Chapter 8 A Word About Faculty and Staff 89

Chapter 9 Exploring Beyond Campus 95

Bibliography 101

Appendix Where to Turn—Additional Resources 103

EDITOR'S PREFACE

The transition to college marks a significant milestone in a person's life. Many of you will be preparing to live away from your friends and family for the very first time. Clearly this is and should be an exciting time.

It is a time to experience new things and experiment with new options. While the opportunity to grow is clear—so too are the many challenges you will experience as you transition from high school to college.

Research suggests that the first year of college is the most difficult period of adjustment a student faces. Not only will you be required to adjust to new academic demands but you will also have to navigate a number of social and emotional challenges that accompany your life as a college student. The books found within this series—*Cognella Series on Student Success*—have been developed to help you with the many issues confronting your successful transition from life as a high school student to life as a collegiate. Each book within the series was designed to provide research-based, yet practical advice to assist you in succeeding in your college experience.

The current book, *A Student's Guide to College Transition*, helps students (and parents) understand that there's more to college than classes. The book highlights the many co-curricular opportunities that are available to students in college and the value of engaging in these opportunities.

In reading this book you will find direction for navigating the many choices available so that they help to make you more attractive (and unique) to potential employers. While the information provided is founded upon good research, the manner in which it is presented is very reader friendly, clear, and practical. The book employs case illustrations in a feature called "*Voices From Campus,*" and opportunities to apply what you are learning in a feature called "*Your Turn.*"

I know that you will find this, as well as the other books within the series, to be a useful guide to your successful transition from high school to college.

Richard Parsons, Ph.D.
Series Editor

THERE'S MORE TO COLLEGE THAN CLASSES

I um, actually thought it would be a lot of parties, you know like in the movies—Old School, Animal House, that kind of thing.

—Mike (Junior year)

In thinking back to what he thought college would be like, Mike realized that perhaps he had gotten a lot of his ideas from the movies. The same might be true for you. You have probably heard, or been told, that college is the best time of your life. Perhaps you have thought about why or have some ideas about what college is like based on stories you have heard from others, movies, TV, or books.

As with most things in life, these stories give you ideas about what to expect, but are often embellished for others to hear. Stories you may have heard from others are usually the extreme stories—meaning the best time the person had or the funniest or perhaps even the worst. And most likely, as with any good storyteller, these have been exaggerated a bit to make for a good story. The same goes for Hollywood—they take a small part of what college may be like (for example, a fraternity) and create a fun, wild, and crazy story to sell it and to get people to come see the movie.

Think about the stories you have heard. Most of them are probably about life outside of class—the social aspects of college. Not too many fun stories or big movies get made about classes and academics. So your expectations about what college will be like are probably based on creative storytelling at best and fantasy at worst.

The social side of college involves more than just hanging out with others, finding lifelong friends, and attending parties. Actually the valuable social side involves a bit more planning and thoughtfulness than any of these things might lead you to believe. That is where this book can help. While your major and what you study is important, how you spend your time outside of class can be just as, if not more, important. With so many people going to college it is often the things you did outside of class that can set you apart in a crowd. It is also these same things that can give you experiences and skills you may not learn in the classroom. So instead of leaving your future up to chance, you might consider thinking about your options before you go. This book will walk you through the various ways you might get involved in college and help you sort through which ones you might want to check out and which ones you are not interested in. Once you get to college there will be a lot to learn and do, but by thinking this through before you get there, you can be a step ahead on day one. Perhaps the following Voices From Campus (1.1) will give you an idea about what you might encounter.

VOICES FROM CAMPUS 1.1

Frank

I couldn't even believe I got an interview. Applying for that job was a long shot, but it was something I really wanted to do, so I figured why not. When I got to the company, the guy who met me sat down to talk. He said, "I saw you volunteered for Habitat for Humanity in college. I did too! Wasn't it a great experience?" Our common experience really created a way for us to talk, and he told me later in the day that it was my involvement in community services, especially Habitat, that made him decide to interview me. The funny thing is, I only did it because my girlfriend at the time dragged me along. (I didn't tell him that.) But after I went a few times I really loved it and continued to be involved even after we broke up. It's so funny how something that seems so random actually landed me my first job.

—Frank

Getting involved at college also helps you be successful while you are in college. That might not make sense, right? How can being busy help you get good grades? Well surprisingly that is exactly what happens. Of course, you can't do everything, but it turns out that those students who are involved tend to do the best in college. It's not just about getting a job after college, but doing well while you are there. There are of course other benefits as well. Students who get involved learn things like leadership, time management, social skills, and confidence. All of these things help you to not only be successful at college, but at work and at life. So hopefully now you are considering that it might be important to do things outside of class at college. But where should you start?

Before you start deciding what you want to do in college, it will be helpful to think about what you did (or did not do) in high school. As suggested by

Maria (see Voices From Campus 1.2), a simple reflection like the one you are asked to consider in Your Turn 1.1. may give you some clarity about what it is that you did in high school and what you find of value. This awareness may result in direction once you get to campus. So spend some time filling out the chart below (see Your Turn 1.1) about what you did when you weren't in class in high school.

VOICES FROM CAMPUS 1.2

Maria

As I filled this out, I realized that the biggest amount of my time was spent on the school newspaper. I liked talking to others about what they saw and what happened, but I didn't like all the time spent writing and editing the story. I learned how to convince others to talk to me and I liked listening to them.

—Maria

YOUR TURN 1.1

Things I Did With My Time

Directions:

Take a moment to reflect upon the things you did with your time (examples might be athletics, band, volunteering, working, youth group, etc.) and the value these activities had for you.

Activity	Why I did this activity	What I liked about it	What I didn't like about it	What I learned from doing it

Having reflected on your out-of-class activities, go back to the chart and think about college. Place a star next to the things you think you might be interested in continuing to do and cross out the things you don't want to do in college. If you are unsure, that is okay, just mark the things you have the strongest feelings about.

Now here is some great news—you don't have to do any of the same things (well you might need to have a job, but it could be a different one and you may decide to do something that you have a scholarship for, like athletics). For the most part, college is a clean slate. Not only that, but college will have a lot of different kinds of things for you to get involved in that didn't exist in your high school. So while thinking about what you did in high school is a good start, it is just that, a place to start. As you think about college, what are some things that you might like to try? Perhaps some things that you wish you had tried but didn't, or things you wish your high school or community had. Or maybe it was something you wanted to do but you couldn't afford the time or cost? It might be something you wanted to learn or an experience you wanted to have. If you make a list of these things, they can serve as "beacons" to guide you through all the choices and possibilities presented on campus in order to engage in those that you find truly compelling or, as in the case of Malcolm (see Voices From Campus 2.3), those that serve as an entry point for new social connections.

VOICES FROM CAMPUS 1.3

Malcolm

When I was in high school there was an anime club, and the stuff those kids did was just so cool. Their drawings, the movies they watched, it was just so interesting. But my friends all made fun of those kids, so there was no way I was going to go to a club meeting. Plus I had plenty of other things to do. I did draw cartoons on my own at home and my uncle always told me they were really good, but I just figured that he had to say that because he was my uncle. Then when I went to college, a kid on my hall was really into anime and I talked to him about it. He said there was a group on campus and invited me to come along. I figured, why not. So I went and it was just like I thought it would be—really creative people drawing, encouraging each other, and hanging out. They didn't all do anime, but they all were into illustration. And it really helped me learn to draw better and gain confidence in my own work. I might not do this for a living, but I got to meet a bunch of people I most likely would have never hung out with and learned a lot about graphic artists and novels that I most certainly would have never known. I am so glad I stepped out of my comfort zone and tried it.

—Malcolm

You may not have as clear an idea as Malcolm did, but hopefully you have thought of at least a few things that you have an interest in doing in college. There are probably other things that you have not even thought about that you could do. We will explore a lot of these options in this book, but for now, pick one thing you starred in your list of high school activities that you think you want to keep doing and one thing on your list of things you are interested in doing.

Now check the website of a college you are considering (or the college you have selected). Use the search engine on the college page to see if you can find out about a club or activity related to your interests. If nothing comes up, then search for clubs and organizations or for student life. If you still can't find anything, that's okay, we will talk more later about the resources on campus that can best help you connect with your interests.

Now that you know both why it's important to get involved and have given some thought as to how you might like to be involved, let's explore some of the things that college has to offer. The rest of this book is broken into sections about the various ways you might get involved. It walks you through each of these possibilities, the things you might consider as you think about getting involved, and gives you practical tips and advice from students about how to explore your options and make the most of your college experience.

1.1: A Special Note for Commuters

Joel

My first year I commuted to campus and I just went to class and left. I had a lot going on and didn't think I could afford the time to get involved. At the beginning of my second year I was required to go to a club for my business 101 class. So I picked the entrepreneurs club. I only went for the class assignment, but then I met a bunch of people I liked and ended up getting involved. Now when I go to campus I feel much more a part of it.

—Joel

Those who commute to campus have some additional choices to make about getting involved. Clubs and organizations often meet at night, student activities can often occur during the weekends, and commuters are often trying to maximize their time on campus by scheduling things close together so they do not have "dead" time in their schedule. When making scheduling decisions commuters often do not think of building in time for extracurricular activities and can miss out on valuable college experiences. If you do decide to commute to campus, all of the information in this book still applies to you. You may have an off-campus job already, but you should still consider working on campus. You might be pressed for time, but you should still get involved on campus because it will have the same benefits that this book discusses.

Additionally, many campuses offer commuter groups so you can connect with others who are commuting. The student life department can point you in the direction of any services or groups geared specifically for commuters. That's a great place to start meeting others, but don't stop there, follow the advice in this book and work to make the most of your college experiences just like other students.

One thing you may not think about as a commuter is where you are going to hang out between classes. The first place people think to study in between classes is the library. This is a great place to go to get work done and connect to resources on campus. But consider other places you might go as well. If you have some gap time and know that you really won't get a lot of studying done in an hour break, consider checking out the student union or other centers on campus. Often campuses have student lounges in various places on campus where you can meet others on campus. When you have lighter reading to do or you just want to talk, you should consider finding a more social place on campus. Check out the signs posted about events, ask questions of other students hanging out (even if you don't have any, this is a great way to meet someone), and just listen to what others are saying to get a feel for what is happening on campus.

1.2: A Special Note for Community College Students

VOICES FROM CAMPUS 1.5

Shondra

Honestly I went to community college to save money, I didn't really even think of it as a real college. But my classes were challenging and it had all the stuff a four-year college would have. I ended up getting involved in the activities club and making some really great friends and connections. Now that I am about to transfer, it's kind of bittersweet. On the one hand I'm excited to finish my degree, but I'll honestly really miss the people I've gotten to know. This school feels more like my home than I ever thought it could be.

—Shondra

You may be thinking of going to a community college for part or all of your college degree. This can be a great choice for a variety of reasons including saving money, figuring out what career you want, or getting an associate degree or certificate that will give you job-related experience and qualifications. Whatever the reason, this book still applies. Community colleges have clubs and organizations, work-study programs, study abroad, community service, and more. Don't think this book isn't for you if you are attending community college—it is.

The nice thing about a community college is that everyone is a commuter, so you won't experience the changes in campus from daytime to nighttime that can happen on residential campuses. Just like in the commuter section above, all the same things apply. Getting involved on campus is just as important at a community college as it is at a four-year school. It can actually have additional benefits in that it can connect you to resources who will be very helpful if you decide to transfer. Getting used to being involved will become a natural part of your college experience and you will get the benefits of involvement including managing your time, so that if you do transfer, you will be used to managing your time effectively and can more seamlessly fit into your new transfer institution.

The other great benefit to being involved at a community college is that you can take on leadership opportunities much faster as the leadership positions are available sooner than they would be at a four-year school. So you can get great experience and résumé builders in your first two years of school. At four-year schools you often have to wait until your junior or senior year to become a leader. If it is very big school, it can be much harder to get a leadership position at all. The one downside about being involved at a community college is that you need to do it quickly. Waiting too long to decide might mean it's time to transfer and you haven't gotten around to doing it yet. So pick something right away and give it a try.

On a final note about community college, we know from research that attending community college full time, for even one semester, leads to greater success. That is because when you are full time you usually get more involved on campus and get all the great rewards we talk about in this book. So consider trying to go full time (15 credits) for at least one semester, this will really help with your success.

1.3: The Take Away

- The social aspects of college are just as important as your classes, and with some thought and planning you can get ahead of the stress of figuring out what you might like to do.

- You have choices about what to do in college that are more diverse than in high school.

- Getting involved can help you succeed both in college by teaching you valuable skills for success and after college through networking and by setting you apart from others.

- If you are a community college student or a commuter, all the advice in this book is still relevant for you, and actually getting involved is the most beneficial to you.

SHOULD I WORK AND IF SO, WHERE?

I didn't really have a choice to work, I had to help with the costs. But I wish I had known I could find a job that supported me as a student. It took until my junior year for me to realize that working off campus was hurting my grades. When I finally got a job on campus in the library, I started to improve my grades, and I also got over my fear of using the library!

—Joelle, Class of 2015

For some students, getting a job in college is non-negotiable. Some students need the extra income to help pay tuition, books, and other expenses. Others have enough financial aid or support that a job is optional. Regardless of your situation, working on campus can provide you with extra income, provide you with work experience, and help you get involved. There can be drawbacks to working while in college as well, so let's take a minute to talk about what work options exist, what the pros and cons are for each, and then help you think through want you might like to do.

2.1: Working On Campus

If you want to work on campus, there are two types of jobs. The first is what is called a work-study job. These jobs are part of your financial aid package from the school. Each school has a different way of assigning these jobs, but if you get a work-study position as part of your aid packet, the sooner you can find out the types of jobs available and how you can get them the better. There are a variety of jobs, so if your school allows you to select and apply for them, doing your homework can help you find the right job for you. If you do not qualify for work-study, there are often jobs on campus that are not part of financial aid. Students are usually hired for these positions during the beginning of the year, so asking about them during the summer before can give you a leg up on your classmates as well. To help you think about what qualities might be important to you, complete Your Turn 2.1 and the ranking of qualities now.

YOUR TURN 2.1

Job Qualities Ranking

In the list below, rank-order what is most important to you in a job, with 1 being most important to 11 being least important.

_____ A flexible schedule

_____ The ability to do homework on my downtime

_____ Meeting peers and interacting with others

_____ Getting experience related to my area of study

_____ Something that challenges my thinking

_____ Something that is repetitive and I do not have to think a lot

_____ A quiet place where I do not have to interact with others

_____ A chance to engage with college administrators or staff

_____ Working during the day M–F

_____ Working nights and weekends

_____ I want my job to be very close to where I live

This list should help you narrow down the types of jobs you want to look for on campus (and you can also use this to prioritize your ideal work environment if you work off campus). Jobs on campus tend to have fairly set hours and are used to students' schedules. They do not expect you to work over school holidays and can be understanding of high pressure times like finals week. For work-study jobs there are limits to the number of hours you can work on campus, so this can help you manage your time. Studies have shown that for many students, working 10–15 hours a week on campus improves their grades. Working more than 15 hours a week tends to have the opposite effect and your grades may start to slip.

Working on campus also helps you meet peers, make relationships with mentors and advisors on campus, and exposes you to opportunities you might not otherwise be aware of as a student.

The exercise in Your Turn 2.1 also provides a good guide as to questions you may want to ask during an interview. While you do not want to ask if you can do homework on the job, you can ask how busy the office is, who you interact with, what the work environment is like, and things that will give you an idea about what the job will be like. If the process for hiring does not start until school starts, you can also ask your orientation advisor or upperclassmen for advice or contacts for jobs on campus. Peers often have a good idea of what it is really like to work in the various jobs on campus.

The student in Voices From Campus 2.1 found out about a potential job and what it was like from his peer advisor.

VOICES FROM CAMPUS 2.1

Mohammad

My peer advisor told me he worked in the dean's office on campus and that because of that he got to meet a lot of the staff who run the activities at the school. Through working there he knew about all the cool things going on before anyone else, so he knew what bands were coming, various speakers, and got to help set up for the spring carnival. He said that now he is the president of the campus activities board and actually gets to pick what bands are coming. That sounds like something I'd like.

—Mohammad

Another advantage of working on campus is that it helps you feel connected to campus and often leads to getting involved. As we discussed in Chapter 1, being involved in campus leads to success at college. Finally, working on campus means that you are close to work and do not have to spend a lot of time commuting, worrying about parking, spending money on transportation, or spending money on a uniform or other job-related expenses.

However, on-campus jobs usually provide low salaries and your hours may be limited. Also it can be hard to find a job you want during your first year since upperclassmen are often in some of the best jobs (they started out just like you, but have moved around in their time there). Maybe you had a job in high school that you can keep if you live close or are commuting or you can get a job related to your interest areas. If you think you want to work off campus, what do you need to know about that?

2.2: Working Off Campus

Your Turn 2.1 can also be helpful to think through what is important to you as you consider a job off campus. There are probably places that typically hire students from your school, so upperclassmen can also be helpful with this. Going to places that often hire students means that they are used to the university schedule and realize you may just be seasonal. Places will often advertise in the school newspaper, put signs up around campus, or send notices to the career services office. The types of jobs in this discussion are not highly skilled jobs such as an internship (see Chapter 3 about internships), but are frequently waitressing, babysitting, retail positions, and tutoring. If you want to branch out and find a job that doesn't usually hire students, you will want to think carefully about your schedule and what you can realistically do.

This student in Voices From Campus 2.2 certainly learned the hard way.

VOICES FROM CAMPUS 2.2

Victor

I got a job as a server at the local restaurant and it was a great way to make money. I was making so much in tips that I said yes anytime someone wanted me to cover for them. Everything was going great until midterms when I got my grades and realized that they were lower than I expected. I went to my advisor and she mapped out with me how many hours a week I was working. Turns out I was working 35 hours a week. No wonder I was struggling in school.

—Victor

Making extra money at an off-campus job can be great, but if it jeopardizes your ability to do well in school, then it isn't worth it. You should also factor in the other costs of working off campus including your commute time and costs. Also make sure you understand your employer's expectations around school holidays. If you are willing to work over the holidays and you are living on campus, you should also check that your residence halls are open over those holidays. Many campuses close their residence halls over breaks, and you could agree to work only to find you have nowhere to live.

Finally a job off campus may not be as flexible for your schedule. Even those employers that hire students may not want to accommodate your finals schedule; after all, they are running a business. Make sure you can commit the time they ask in the ways they ask for it. Doing poorly in a job, being fired, or leaving an employer in a jam is never a good idea.

2.3: Above All Do a Good Job

Jobs can lead to work experience and references, both vital to future employment opportunities after college. Regardless of what job you get, it is important to do a good job, communicate with your supervisor, show up on time, and represent yourself well. You never know when someone you work for might know of another opportunity, might have a connection in a field you are interested in, or might get called for a reference. Jason, a current high level executive in New York, got his first job out of college from his job as a waiter.

VOICES FROM CAMPUS 2.3

Jason

I was a waiter for three years during college and I had some regulars. I always made sure to know their names, serve them well, and do a good job. The last semester of my senior year one of them said, "Jason, what are you doing when you graduate?" I replied that I didn't know; I was still looking. He said he had been watching me for three years now and that he knew what a good job I do. He asked me to apply to work at his company. I did just that and got the job. That was 18 years ago and I've gone on to work for an international company doing the job of my dreams.

—Jason

2.4: The Take Away

- Working on campus has many advantages as these jobs are created specifically for students.

- Finding out about the types of jobs available and how to apply for them as early as possible will help you get a better choice of jobs.

- Knowing what you want in a job can really help you decide where to apply.

- If you work off campus, make sure you set limits on your time and consider all the pros and cons before committing.

- If you work during college, always do an excellent job. You never know where it might lead.

WORK EXPERIENCE OPPORTUNITIES

From being an RA I learned how to manage conflict, stay calm in crisis, plan events, and stay on top of paperwork. I just did it to get a free room, but then I ended up loving it and learning so much!

—Maliek (Senior year)

I n the last chapter we talked about both on-campus and off-campus jobs. Those are just two of the many work opportunities available to you while in college. There are other types of work, some paid and some not paid, that can give you job experience and help you build skills and connections for your career after college. Some of these opportunities include internships, research, externships, and paid student leadership positions.

3.1: Internships

Some schools offer internships through what they call co-ops. These are specific semesters where you actually do not take classes and instead work full time. The school is involved in helping you set them up, you get credit for them, and they are required to graduate. If this is something you think you might be interested in, look for a school that specifically requires a co-op experience. At schools where co-ops are not required, there are still opportunities to do work related to your job in the form of internships. Internships are different from a job in that they are related directly to your field and are for a defined amount of time. Employers are increasingly looking for students who have done internships.

The career development office on your campus is the place to go to inquire about internships. Internships can be available at any time, but often students do them during the summer. Some schools offer credit for internships, others do not. You will have to check your school's policy regarding internships. While getting as much work experience as you can is helpful, it can be difficult to get an internship after your first year of college. Companies generally are looking for students who have already completed some classes related to their field, so many students do their internships the summer after their junior year. This does not mean that you should not go to career development and explore opportunities prior to this. Actually, you should go to career development during your first semester and start planning your time at college. They can help you map out what you'd like to do and the best times to do it. You can also find out how to find out about job, career and internship opportunities. You never know when your ideal experience will become available. They can also help you understand all of the things you will need to think through as you work to get an internship, including your social media presence, creating a cover letter and résumé, how to network, and more.

Before we talk more about internships, spend a few minutes exploring how career development can help with internships by completing Your Turn 3.1.

YOUR TURN 3.1

Career Development Exploration

Go the career development website of the school you attend or the one you want to attend (the easiest way to find it is to go to the school's website and search for career development).
Find the link related to internships.

- Do they offer a timeline on applying for internships? If so, what are key dates?

- Who in the office coordinates internships and how do you make an appointment with them?

- Do they give credit for internships?

- What else did you read that you found interesting?

Now do an Internet search for internships in _____ (field you are thinking about studying).

- What kinds of things came up?

- What types of companies are offering internships?

- When do you have to apply?

- Do they list any requirements about the number of classes you have had or what year in college they prefer?

- Are there any experiences they want you to have before you apply?

There are some additional things you will want to think about as you explore internships. You may have no idea what you want to major in, let alone the type of internship you want. That is okay. By exploring the types of internships your school can connect you to, you can begin to think about other things you might want to do. Sometimes an internship can help you in ways you do not expect (see Voices from Campus 3.1).

VOICES FROM CAMPUS 3.1

Amber

The summer of my junior year I did an internship at a local bank. As an accounting major I really thought I wanted to be in banking. Spending a summer doing it helped me realize that while I like accounting, I want to use it in a way that is part of an organization that is helping people not just managing money. It was not what I thought an internship would do for me, but I'm glad I know that now versus getting my first job and realizing I didn't like it. Now I can do some volunteer work my senior year and really change my job search strategy.

—Amber

As the time approaches there will be other things you need to consider, including whether you can do an internship for free or not and whether you want to do an internship near home, near your college, or in some other location (for instance some fields like film offer the best internships in New York and Los Angeles). Finally, while it may be a way off, it never hurts to start thinking about people who might be able to help you land an internship. Take a minute now to think about who those people might be by completing Your Turn 3.2.

YOUR TURN 3.2

People I Might Be Connected To

Sometimes getting an internship only through a position posting can be limiting. You are competing with a lot of other students applying for the same jobs. Just like in your job search after college, it is often connections that can help you get an internship. You might think you do not know anyone who might be helpful or in the field you are interested in, but you never know. As you think about the type of job you might like to do, list some people in your community who might know someone who works in that field. Keep this list handy when you want to talk to people about a summer job or internship. You might be surprised at how many people want to help you, after all most people had someone help them at some point.

Job/Field/Career	Person I know	Connected to whom
Sports management	Friend's mom	Works as an usher at the sports arena
Law	Uncle	College roommate is a lawyer

Research is another interesting opportunity at many colleges that can give you great experience in your field. Right now you might only think of that as something you do to write a paper, but it's much bigger than that and has a lot of benefits.

3.2: Research

Faculty at colleges do research in their area of study all the time. It's how they keep current in their field, how new knowledge is generated, and how new inventions are created. We often think of research just in science, but research happens in every field. More and more colleges are working to get undergraduates involved in research. Sometimes these can be paid positions like work-study in Chapter 1 (most often a research assistant) or they can be projects to give you the chance to try research for the first time. If you intend to go to graduate school, it is something you will most definitely be doing. By trying it as an undergrad, you can get exposure to it to see if you like it as well as build up your graduate school application.

Beyond that, it helps you understand your class readings, the ideas in your field, and develops your critical thinking. It is also a great way to make connections with faculty and learn from them one on one. Having strong relationships with faculty has been shown to help students be successful in both grades and graduation. For those applying to graduate school, it provides them with a great academic reference. It can also expose you to things you might never have had a chance to do (e.g., archeological digs, helping to write a book, reading historical documents, understanding political polling technology, developing methods for water purification in underdeveloped countries). It's a chance to put your learning into practice. Another chance to put your learning into practice is an externship.

3.3: Externship

Externships are not as commonly promoted and arranged by colleges as internships, but if you are interested in having one the career development office can help set these up as well. They are shorter opportunities to learn about various jobs and careers and can last anywhere from one day to a few weeks. They often take the form of shadowing and help students to get a look at what it might be like to do a particular job. Unlike an internship, externships do not last a long time, are not for college credit, can be done multiple times, and can be done at any time during your college experience. You can do an externship starting your first year of college. This can be especially helpful if you are undeclared, want to see multiple perspectives on what a career in your field is like, want to increase your network of people, or cannot afford to do an unpaid internship and have difficulty finding a paid one. They are ideal to do over breaks where you can fit them into a week.

VOICES FROM CAMPUS 3.2

Aruna

I had this class that was required for my major, but I totally did not want to take it. As part of it we had to do a two-week externship on marketing at the zoo. I was thinking, "How lame. Everyone knows we have a zoo. They will either come or they won't." I also felt like it was just one more thing to add to my busy schedule. But while working behind the scenes at the zoo I realized just how important their work is. I know it sounds dumb, but I just had not thought about how much research they did there and how important it was in terms of helping save endangered species. I guess it made me want to look at scientific research more and how marketing can help get their message out.

—Aruna

3.4: Paid Leadership Positions

There are usually some paid positions on campus that involve some type of leadership. These positions tend to be more competitive and require higher-level skills than some of the basic on-campus jobs. These can vary by campus but some might include being a resident assistant, student admissions representative, peer advisor, or technology assistant. Some larger campuses also pay their student government boards.

These positions often require flexible hours, training time before the start of the semester, the ability to manage your peers, to work independently, and to work with administration. While they require more time than other on-campus jobs, they also provide the chance to build important job skills that you might not get in an hourly work-study or off-campus job. You are put in charge of projects, expected to make decisions, and trusted with valuable information. The ability to do well in these types of jobs will not only increase your skills for your future career but will also provide you with the opportunity to learn about yourself, which in turn can help you be more successful in college. The training provided for these jobs is given by professionals in their field, and you get the chance to learn new skills and practice them in a fairly risk-free environment with a lot of support and coaching from full-time administration and staff. These positions are not usually open to first-year students, so once you get on campus, keep an eye open for these types of positions and ask upperclassmen about what might exist on your campus.

3.5: The Take Away

- Internships are an important tool to get experience and increase your marketability for future employers.

- It is never too early to talk to the college career development office to think about when you would like to do an internship.

- Doing research as an undergraduate is a highly valuable experience, especially if you plan to attend graduate school.

- Paid student leadership positions are an excellent way to develop solid career skills while also providing you with the opportunity to grow personally and get training in a variety of areas.

LIFE OUTSIDE THE UNITED STATES

STUDY ABROAD

My only regret so far in life is not studying abroad in college.

—April, Class of 1991, author of this book

If you have not considered study abroad or you do not think you will do it while in college, regardless of the reason, keep reading. There is a large variety in studying abroad including when, for how long, if you need to know a language and where you can study abroad. So before you rule it out, consider reading this chapter to make sure you understand all the options. If you have already decided you want to study abroad, this chapter can give you additional things to consider, questions to ask, and expand your view of what that experience could look like. When thinking of studying abroad, most students think of a traditional semester studying and living in another country. While this is a popular option, it is not the only one. Study abroad is not a vacation. You are not going just to have fun (which you will). You will get a unique opportunity to live in another country, something that is harder to do as adult in terms of time, money, and travel restrictions. In many countries, student visas, especially for Americans, are much easier to obtain for longer time periods than general travel for vacation.

Before you read any further, test your knowledge about study abroad in this short quiz.

YOUR TURN 4.1

Test your Knowledge about Study Abroad

So what do you know about study abroad? Answer the questions below and then read on to find out the answers.

	True	False	Depends on your school or program
Study abroad is only offered during the academic year for a semester			
You must speak the language of the country you will be studying in			
Colleges charge an extra fee for studying abroad			
If you are a pre-med or a major with a lot of required classes, you cannot study abroad			

	True	False	Depends on your school or program
If your school does not have a study abroad office, then you cannot study abroad			
When you study abroad you live in a dorm with students from the country where you are studying			
All study abroad opportunities are credit-bearing classes taken at another university			

4.1: Reasons to Go

When you go on vacation you do not really get to know a place. It's like visiting a friend's house for lunch. You can meet their family, see where they live, learn a little about them from conversation, but you really don't know your friend or their family in any depth. If someone were to ask you questions about their family, you would be hard pressed to give anything but the most basic answers. When you study abroad, it's like living with your friend instead of just going for lunch. You can really immerse yourself in the country, the culture, and the people. You will gain a rich and complex understanding of the country from talking to various people, exploring different areas, and learning about its history. An added benefit is that in doing so you learn more about yourself and the world. Things that you thought were just "normal" or common are actually American. Perspectives on what is the right thing to do, what people do for fun, and how they view Americans will make you more aware of your own country and your own beliefs and values.

From a practical perspective studying abroad is also something that will make you stand out in a crowded job market. With the increased diversity in the United States and the global economy, employers want people who have had diverse experiences and who are not afraid to relate to those different than themselves. By choosing to study abroad, you demonstrate that you are able to work with people from other countries and that you are open to new experiences. Your skills as a critical thinker and a creative problem solver increase because you are exposed to new ideas and ways of thinking. It can also build your confidence as you learn to navigate in a foreign country.

It also increases your social and career network of people and opportunities. Whether you are studying with other Americans from across the country, international students who are also studying abroad, or the students from the country where you live, you will have new places to stay when you travel, new connections to regions of the country, and friends who have an entirely different set of friends from your own.

Finally, as mentioned in the introduction, studying abroad in college offers a unique chance to live abroad that is unlike any you will most likely have the rest of your life. You may choose to work abroad, but even then your schedule will not be one of a student. As a student you have a lot of freedom in between classes to explore and a lot of time that is unstructured. This is one of the few times in your life that you will be so unencumbered by outside demands on your time.

4.2: Concerns You May Have

Even with all the benefits, you may still have some questions. Maybe you are concerned about the cost, your class requirements, your language skills, safety, or missing out on activities while you are gone. Let's explore each of these here.

One common question that students have about study abroad is, "How much will it cost?" Students often perceive they cannot afford to study aboard. It does depend on the school, but most schools try to keep the actual cost of attendance the same as if you stayed on campus. Most likely the tuition and room are the same, but there are additional costs for travel to and from the country. And of course if you want to travel on your own, those trips are not included. If money is a concern, there are a few things that you can consider in exploring study abroad options. For a full study abroad semester there are federal scholarships and grants; you may also find scholarships for studying abroad. Each person's circumstances are different, so you will need to do some research to find out more about these options. You can also select a country that is less expensive or go on a shorter trip (keep reading for more information about that).

Fear of missing out is also something that can keep students from studying abroad. Some campuses have certain traditions that happen during a student's time on campus, and those who are involved on campus fear missing out on these traditions or are worried about being able to take on leadership opportunities on campus if they are away during the election or hiring period. This is a legitimate concern; however, if you plan ahead you can ask about doing a video interview for internships, hiring, or other things that may be occurring while you are abroad. In today's global marketplace, video interviews and meetings are commonplace. You may be surprised at how supportive your school can be. Map out your college journey, you can plan ahead and anticipate what is important for you to do to make sure you do not miss any opportunities while you are away.

Most residence life offices will also work with you to arrange housing options when you return (if you plan to live on campus). Contact them as you consider studying abroad.

VOICES FROM CAMPUS 4.1

Jessica

Before I studied abroad I asked the residence life department about interviewing to be an RA because I would be abroad while the process happened. They let me interview before I left and then Skyped with me to ask some follow-up questions. I was on a poor Internet connection in a café in Kenya, but they loved that I was having this experience. So in the end I think it helped me get the RA job.

—Jessica

It is true that life on campus will go on without you. Your friends will have fun without you and you may miss out on some memories. With today's technology you can easily keep in touch through free phone apps and social media. Also remember that you will be gaining even more friends while you are away and making new memories of your own.

Some majors such as pre-med, nursing, or other majors with a lot of required classes can make study abroad during the traditional semester a challenge. This idea often gets perpetuated by other students who tell first-year students that they cannot study abroad. Before you believe everything your peers tell you, it is important to talk to your academic advisor and/or the study abroad office. If your study abroad options will not include the classes you need for your major, you can also explore taking classes at another college or university near your home over the summer. If none of these seem like an option, consider alternative ways to study abroad discussed later in this chapter.

Michael

I always wanted to study abroad. But since I am just not good at languages, I assumed I couldn't study abroad. Then my friend told me she was going to Australia to study marine biology, and I realized that I could go to someplace that spoke English. But even that was wrong, my other friend went to Rome and all her classes were in English. I know it sounds stupid, but I just thought I had to know the language.

—Michael

If you are concerned that you do not speak a foreign language, do not worry. There are three solutions to this problem. The first is to study in a country that speaks English. But you may have interest in a country where English is not the primary language. There are some programs that offer classes in English even though they are based in a country that does not speak English. The downside of this type of program is that you often have classes and live exclusively with other Americans and can miss some of the cultural learning that happens with study abroad. The upside is that you can study abroad in some very interesting places. Finally you can learn to speak the language of the country as your study abroad experience. Language intensive classes tend to be shorter than a full semester or are offered over the summer, so they might look a bit different than a semester study abroad, but you will get the benefits of study abroad and learn a language (or advance your knowledge of one) as well.

In today's globalized connected information age, we often get news from around the world about terror attacks or other news from foreign countries. Like with any travel, you should check with the government about travel advisories. Colleges and universities also monitor countries where their students study and are constantly in touch with programs to make sure things are safe. Before you assume a country is unsafe, do your homework. Remember that the news shows extreme examples of situations and, just like in the United States where we have school shootings and other horrible events, it does not mean the whole country is unsafe. Check the facts as you make a decision about where you might study and what the crime rates are and compare it to U.S. crime rates.

4.3: Options for When to Go

So up to this point we have discussed reasons you may or may not choose to study abroad. As mentioned at the beginning of this chapter, studying abroad for a semester or a year is one way to study abroad, but not the only way. If you cannot take a whole semester away, consider other ways to get an abroad experience—some of these may be for credit, others are not. While traditionally students have gone abroad their junior or senior year, that is changing and schools are offering more and more options to study abroad. There are also shorter trips offered as part of a class over breaks or January and May terms. These one-week to three-week classes do not offer the same in-depth learning experience as a semester-long program but they still provide an opportunity to experience another country in a unique way.

For those who have academic class requirements during the year, the summer is another study abroad option. In addition there are increasingly international internship opportunities over the summer and some jobs teaching English over the summer as well (see countries and visa requirements). In addition schools offer service trips and volunteer opportunities abroad over breaks, and there are non-profits looking for short-term international volunteers. While these options are not all credit bearing, they are a great way to learn about and experience a different culture.

If your school does not have an extensive study abroad office or opportunities it does not necessarily mean you cannot study abroad. Just like you can take classes at other colleges or universities and transfer those credits, these same options often exist for study abroad.

If the idea of going to only one country isn't appealing to you, then there are others options out there including Semester at Sea and SEA semester. See your study abroad or advising office to see if they know of other options or spend some time searching online.

4.4: Things to Consider When Selecting a Study Abroad Experience

If you do decide to study abroad, how do you select where to go and what to study? This will of course be done in conjunction with your advisor and your college or university, but there are some things you should consider as you work to narrow down your options.

Credits and area of study—Is there a college or university that specializes in your field of study? Just like there are top faculty and experts in various areas in the United States, other countries have top universities and scholars in specific fields. Depending on your interest area within your major, studying abroad might also give you the chance to take classes on topics not offered at your school.

Experiential opportunities—Every major has opportunities to experience things in a hands-on way. If you are a theater or English major, imagine studying in England and watching shows at the Globe Theater. Perhaps you're a business major; studying in Hong Kong would expose you to world banks that are not headquartered in the United States. How about studying fashion in Milan or Paris? Make sure you find out what experiential learning opportunities will happen in your studies or on your trip.

Language—Will you be required to take language classes of some type while you study abroad?

Residence—Every study abroad program has a different arrangement for where you will live. This will have a big impact on your experience, so you should ask about what the housing will be like. Will you have a home stay with a host family? Will you be living on campus with other students in the host country or staying with other international students?

VOICES FROM CAMPUS 4.3

Julia

So many people had conflicting opinions about what was better, to stay in a dorm with all Americans or to stay with a host family. I didn't know what to do, but in the end my program had the first half of the semester in a dorm and the second half with a host family. Both were great experiences for different reasons. I think I learned more about the country with the family, but I also got a lot of new friends from across the country while living with other Americans.

—Julia

Transfer credits—Your campus advisor can give you information about transferring credits. But do not assume anything; make sure you do your homework to understand what will transfer and when, how to fill out the paperwork, and what questions you need to ask. If you are doing a study abroad through another university, it is very important to find all this out before you go.

Application time and study time—Every school will have its own process for applying for study abroad. This includes the school you are coming from and the school you are traveling to. In addition, not every class you take will be offered every semester so find out what classes will be offered when as you plan your academic schedule.

Country and time of year—You should make sure you find out about the countries you are interested in. What is the weather like? Are there particular cultural events or celebrations you may be interested in being there for? What is daily life like in the country? Also consider where the university is located. Do not assume that city life or country life in another country is similar to the United States. It is important to understand what the community around the university is like, including where you might shop, how you will get around, how safe it is to travel alone, and how well you need to know the language to get around.

Finances—Aside from traveling to the country, what other expenses will there be? What do you like to do for fun and how much will those same things cost in the country you are traveling to?

Ability to travel to other places—Studying abroad can be a launching place to travel to other countries. For instance plane travel within Europe is relatively inexpensive. If you want to take weekends away or go to the country early or stay beyond your experience, what are the options and costs to do so?

There is a lot to consider, so start thinking about study abroad early. Talk to your advisor, the study abroad office, and upperclassmen who have studied abroad. They can be very helpful in creating a plan that will work for you.

4.5: The Take Away

- Studying abroad will teach you about yourself as well as make you more interesting as a job applicant.
- The answers to Your Turn 4.1 were all false! Hopefully you learned about the various options for study abroad and that one size does not fit all.

you cannot study abroad.

COMMUNITY SERVICE

My parents wanted me to be pre-med and so I was. It sounded like a fine plan and I liked it okay, but then I started tutoring kids through our community service office and I fell in love with teaching. I literally plan my class schedule around when I can tutor next, so it's nice to have found my passion.

—Heng (Junior year)

C ommunity service is more than helping people, it's an opportunity to learn about your community, your neighbors, and ultimately yourself. There are many ways to participate in community service while you are in college. You might do community services as part of orientation, a class, a club, or an organization that does a day of service, an immersive one-day or multiple-day experience, or you could join a group whose whole focus is on community service. Some colleges even have work-study positions doing community service. In this chapter we will explore why you might do service and ways to get involved in service trips and clubs and organizations that focus on service.

5.1: Why Do Service?

Some people grow up learning that service is important. For others, community service and volunteering is something they have never done before. Good news! Unlike so many other things in life, no matter whether you have experience or not, community service is for everyone. So why do it? There are many reasons, but here are a few:

1. *Learning outside the classroom.* You will have many classes that examine problems in the world. You will learn theories about why these problems exist, read about various solutions, and learn about how various people throughout history have approached solving these problems. Reading and learning about something is very important, however getting involved in the problem by seeing it first hand gives you a much richer perspective and experience. Reading about how inner-city schools are not educating students well and learning the historical, social, and political situations that have created this problem is one thing, but going into a school and tutoring the kids will give you an entirely different perspective.

VOICES FROM CAMPUS 5.1

Camila

We are studying economic policy in my econ class and while it's interesting, it's so philosophical that I can get bored with it. That changed when I signed up for a Habitat trip over spring break to go help build houses in Appalachia. That really opened my eyes to how important economic policy is and the ways it really shapes politics and people's lives.

—Camila

2. *Feel good about yourself.* Helping others makes you feel better. Research is pretty clear on this—when you support others, it boosts your self-esteem and overall feelings about yourself.

3. *You help others.* This seems obvious, but it really does benefit others—even if it is something like stuffing envelopes. Non-profits do not have a lot of resources, and help of any kind is appreciated and needed.

4. *Learn diverse perspectives.* Human nature often creates a desire to hang out with, seek out, and meet people who are like us. Whether on social media, in the dining hall, or in class, we tend to gravitate to those who are the most like us. This helps us feel safe and reinforces our idea of ourselves. Those who agree with us are easier to be around and confirm our beliefs about the world. However, the world is a diverse place and community service exposes you to different people and ideas than you may get in your everyday life. This helps you understand yourself better (you can examine why you think the way you do), you can see how others understand things, and you can begin to see a variety of ways to do things, solve problems, and approach situations. This makes you better at your schoolwork, a

better employee (and candidate in job searches), and will help you adjust to new things in life more easily.

Jonah

I didn't really think about how I had only been interacting with people my own age while I was in college, but then I did tutoring and not only did I get to meet some pretty fun kids, but I also met some people who have lived in this community their whole lives. It really changed my perspective on this area of the country and I got some adult perspectives (from people other than my professors and parents) that really made me think.

—Jonah

5. *Meet other people.* This is similar to #4 above, but goes a step further than just learning about new perspectives. Working side by side with people creates opportunities to get to know them. Working towards a common goal creates a bond and friendship over time.

So hopefully now you are thinking that maybe you should at least try community service when you get to college, or continue to do some type of service if you have already been involved in service before. If you have been involved in service previously, it was probably through an established group or organization who chose the activity for you—whether that was your family, your church, or high school. Now that you are in college, your choice of how to be involved is yours and the options are more varied. Before you read about the different ways you can get involved, take some time to think about the types of things you would like to do.

YOUR TURN 5.1

Exploring interest areas and type of work

1. Check off all that apply.

I am most likely to click on stories about....

_____ Animals

_____ The environment

_____ Hunger

_____ Children

_____ The elderly

_____ Housing

_____ Education

_____ Political action organizations

_____ Healthcare

_____ War, peace, or gun issues

Others _____

_____

This list might help answer this question: When you think about things you would like to change in the world, what are you most passionate about?

So now that you have an idea about the type of organization you might be interested in joining, the type of service you will be doing is also important to consider.

2.   Rank the following from most like you to least like you:

_____ I like to see immediate results from my work.

_____ I like to work with my hands.

_____ I like to work behind the scenes to make changes in policies and laws that will help others.

_____ I like to work behind the scenes to help an organization serve its mission.

_____ I like working directly with people.

_____ I like working with a group to make a difference.

_____ I like helping animals.

Other things you can think of:

_____

_____

_____

_____

These are not mutually exclusive (meaning you can like a few equally), but they can provide some help as you think about combining what you like to do with the types of service you want to do. For instance, if you like helping people directly, then working at a soup kitchen where you serve meals or tutoring kids might be for you. But if you want to see immediate results and work with your hands, cleaning up a neighborhood or building a house or a playground might be more your speed. This list can serve as a starter for asking questions about how you will be spending your time when you volunteer with an organization. It's okay to have preferences. You should do something you like to do so that you have a positive attitude and want to participate.

Your college might not have every opportunity listed above, but knowing your interests is helpful. Below are the various ways that service opportunities (aside from ones you do as part of a different group) are offered in college.

5.2: Service Clubs

College and universities often have clubs on campus that focus on community service and that are student run. These groups function much like the student clubs and organizations we will discuss in Chapter 6. They have regular meetings, club officers, and regularly planned activities.

These clubs can include a variety of service activities from tutoring to building houses with Habitat for Humanity to prison outreach and elderly outreach (these are just a few examples). You can find out about these clubs through orientation or the student life office. The value of being involved in one of these is that it provides a structured way for you to be involved in service. The student life office, or students involved in the group can tell you the level and frequency of service they expect. In addition to helping others, you can find others who have common interests and goals. Additionally, it provides opportunities for leadership either on a project basis or as a club officer once you have been involved for a while. This type of service (unlike service trips) has no monetary cost in order to participate in as your involvement is covered by a student activities fee. The downside to being a part of a service group is that you may not feel sure you can commit to their time demands or you may just want to do service rather than participate in the other club expectations like weekly meetings. If you find yourself just wanting to sign up for service opportunities without a formal student group, there are often other places on campus who organize service days or experiences (e.g., campus ministry organizations or an office of community service). If you are concerned about your ability to manage your time or balance service with your schoolwork but are still interested in doing community service, there are some ways you can do a more intensive service trip over breaks and summers. These can have the added benefit of travel and intensive team building—a quick way to make really great friends.

5.3: Service Trips

Colleges often offer trips over holidays or spring breaks (commonly referred to as alternative spring break). Going on a trip over a break can be an amazing experience. These are usually short trips where you travel with a group of students from your school and perform some sort of community service. The project may be local (within the community where you attend college) regional, national, or even international.

VOICES FROM CAMPUS 5.3

Frank

I did alternative spring break with Habitat for Humanity and we went to the Ninth Ward of New Orleans. It was so totally cool and fun. I met some great people from my school that I didn't know and got to talk to some residents of the city. Even though hurricane Katrina was a while ago, there were still so many homes that had not been rebuilt. Working with the local chapter of Habitat we not only learned about how to help with basic building, but we learned the history of the area, what happened after the flood, and what is happening now in the area. It really blew my mind.

—Frank

The value in these trips is really more for the people going than for those you are going to help, so you might think carefully about the trip. Some service staff have given the wise advice that if you wouldn't do the trip if you were not with students from your college or you wouldn't do it without your phone to document and post about it, then maybe you shouldn't do it. Oftentimes the funds you have to raise to send yourself on one of these trips might serve the people in the community better if they just received the money and were allowed to spend it to improve their community as they see fit. There is however a growing awareness of these issues and concerns, so those running service trips are becoming more involved with local agencies and community members to make sure there is value not only for the students but for the community they are serving. If you decide to consider one of these trips, ask the following questions:

- Are we working with an established organization within the community?
- Are we offering a true skill or something the community needs?
- Does the community we are working in want us there?
- Has the community requested assistance and are we approaching this trip as taking their lead or are we assuming we know what is best for a community other than our own?

Another factor for these types of trips is that they involve fundraising of some type. Unlike community service through an organization on campus, the cost of running these trips adds up when you have to cover travel, lodging, and food. Students are encouraged to raise funds on campus through bake sales, car washes, and all sorts of creative endeavors. Some set up GoFundMe pages or other social media campaigns and use it as an additional opportunity to learn about non-profit fundraising. If you are someone who is shy about asking for money, make sure you understand completely what you are signing up for when you agree to do a service trip. Aside from the fundraising, make sure you are comfortable with the lodging (often sleeping on a church floor) and other arrangements. These can be a great way to have fun while helping others; just make sure you are up for the adventure.

If you want a trip longer than a holiday or spring break or you want a trip that is not associated with your college, there are other options for summer community service. The career services office, community service office, or other online resources can be good places to start.

5.4: The Take Away

- There is no experience needed to do community service, so don't be shy.

- Community service is more than just helping others, you will learn about yourself and the world in interesting and profound ways.

- Do services based on both your interest areas as well as how you like to spend your time or what you are good at.

- As you plan your time in college and think about service, consider the various options for service. It can be a regular part of your schedule or you can do service as part of a special program over a break.

- Consider the needs of the community and what you can learn from those you are working with to make the most of your experience.

CLUBS AND ORGANIZATIONS

I picked up a flyer at the club and organization fair during orientation and ended up going to a meeting for the campus political action group. I really just did it to meet people, but one thing led to another and during my junior year I was the president. Now I get to meet all sorts of interesting people on campus, bring in speakers, and have learned how to lead a meeting. It's been pretty cool.

—Tanisha (Junior year)

Joining a student group of any kind has so many benefits. We know from students' personal stories, their GPAs, and their graduation data that involved students do better in college than those that are not involved. So it's not a question of whether you should join a club or organization, but which ones and how many. There are some exceptions of course. If you are involved on campus in something other than a club—whether it is athletics, research, work-study, or some type of activity where you are spending time with staff, faculty, and peers, then you are getting the benefits of being involved from those activities. However, even being in just one club or organization can open a whole world of new friends, leadership experiences, and résumé and network builders. It can also get you a lot of free T-shirts. There are a variety of clubs and organizations. Some we have already covered (like community service) and others we will cover in later chapters (like athletic clubs). Every campus has different options, but one thing is for sure, if you want to be in a club, there is something to meet your interests.

6.1: How Do You Find Out About Them?

Most colleges have some type of activities fair at the beginning of the semester where current clubs set up tables in the quad or some other central location. This is a great way to meet other club members and hear about what they do and when they meet. It can also be very overwhelming. The students at each table will often ask for your contact info and will hand you info about their group. It can be tempting to take each flyer, but often those flyers end up in the trash. While you do not want to over plan your time at the fair, you should think about what you are looking for in a club or organization before you go. You might also consider taking a picture of the flyer or information from the groups you are most interested in, that way you won't need to worry about losing the flyer and the picture will be in your phone to remind you to follow up. When classes start you can be a bit overwhelmed and forget all your great ideas about getting involved, so having that reminder in your phone can be helpful when you realize you really meant to follow the advice in this book and get involved! There are a few things you can do before attending the fair to maximize the experience. First, you can go to the college website and search for clubs and organizations to see what they have. If nothing comes up, try student life, student activities, or student affairs. They are the departments who oversee these groups.

Before you go you should also consider why you are getting involved and what you want to get out of the experience.

YOUR TURN 6.1

Goals for Involvement

Throughout this book you have been asked to identify your interests and reflect on things you have done in the past. Look back to Your Turn 1.1 to remind yourself about why you did the activities you did in high school as well as your reflections about what you liked, what you learned, etc. Some of the reasons you did things in high school might be similar to your motivations in college, but some of your goals may have changed. In high school you make friends in clubs, but you might also have been thinking about college and what might look good on your application. In college, some of those goals for being in a club are the same as high school, like making friends, but some are different. Many students feel it's too early to know what they want to do after college. Other students think they know, but that might change during college. And a few students know exactly what they want to do and it will not change. Regardless of whether you think you know your exact path, you will most likely do one of two things after you graduate—get a job (or do some type of volunteer work) or go on to more schooling like graduate, law, or medical school. You may stay in the area where you attended college, move back home (or stay home if you commute), or move someplace you have never been. College helps prepare you not only for your career or more school, it prepares you for life. You will learn how to manage your time, deal with conflict, lead others, make life choices, and manage your money. For most of these things, you learn them outside of class. You may not have thought about this before, but you learn many practical life and job skills by being involved on campus in clubs and organizations. These are the place where you can try new things with little risk, learn from your peers, and get hands-on advice and skills.

By thinking about what you want to do after college you can work backwards to think about how you can get there. In *A Student's Guide to a Meaningful Carrer*, this series, you will explore career choices, but right now, think about life choices.

Fill out this chart below

Things I'm good at	Things I'm not good at	Things I like	Things I don't like

YOUR TURN 6.2

Secondly, create a list of jobs or careers you think you might be interested in and then what skills you think you'll need to do those jobs. If you don't know, do an Internet search, talk to your guidance counselor, or even email someone doing that job and ask them.

Jobs	Skills I need
Sports Management	multi-taking Making client feel important Negotiating

When you go to the club fair, consider joining clubs that will help you improve the items you noted in the "Things I'm not good at" and the "Skills I need" columns.

6.2: Picking the Magic Number: How Many Clubs Should I Join?

With so many to choose from, how do you decide which ones to get involved in and how many? While there is no right answer for everyone, there are a few guidelines to consider as you decide: What type of activities are you interested in? What are your goals for involvement? How much time do you want to spend (or how much time do you think you'll have to spend)? In addition to these three questions, which we will discuss below, here is some general advice for picking what to do.

General Advice

There is no one-size-fits-all activity. What you choose to get involved in will vary greatly depending on your responses to your turn 6.1 and 6.2. I would recommend however that you think about your involvement in three different clubs.

1.   Find a group that matches both your interest and passion. This will help you find a group of people who you feel comfortable with and where you know you will want to spend time.

2.   Join a group that is a bit out of your comfort zone or something you have always wanted to try. College is a great time to stretch yourself and try something new for little to no cost. Once you are out of college you won't have as much time to try new things and you may not have the opportunity, time, or money. For instance if you have thought you might like hiking, join the outdoors club.

3.   You should consider joining an academic club. Once you know your major, you should find out what clubs or organizations exist around your area of interest. (It may not be directly related to your major, but there are often groups that have focuses that would include your major. For instance, there might not be an accounting club but there might be a business club.)

Types of Club

There are many different types of clubs and groups (see the list on page 60 for a listing of the types). Look over the types and compare it to what you did in Your Turn 1.1 in chapter one where you reflected on what you did with your time in High School. Also think about the three types of clubs listed above to narrow down your interests.

Goals

Hopefully you did the exercise in Your Turn 6.1. If not, reconsider and do that now. This exercise hopefully expanded your ideas about the reasons to join a club beyond just social opportunities. While you are certainly going to make friends, there are other reasons you might consider joining a club. Even meeting people can be about more than just getting new friends. The chance to create a network of people who have common interests or goals can be helpful not only in college but once you graduate. Other goals you might have for joining a group could include learning a new skill, broadening the diversity of your friend group, increasing skills, and developing leadership.

You probably had a group of friends and activities in high school that became the hub of your social life. You hung out with the same group and did the same type of things as they did. This group was a great support for you in high school and most likely you will stay in touch with some of them during and after college. Depending on your high school you may have had a lot of choices for clubs or limited choices. But college is a place where you can learn new things and try out different things with little risk. So instead of just sticking with what you know, this is your chance to try something new.

6.3: Time Involved

VOICES FROM CAMPUS 6.1

Todd

Wow, I remember going to the first club meeting and they listed off all these meetings and activities and I was like, whoa, no way am I doing this. On my way out of the meeting, a club member came over and introduced himself. I was straight with him, I was like, "It's not gonna happen. I just can't do all that stuff." He laughed and told me that I didn't have to do it all. He said I could do as much or as little as I liked. So I decided to pick one thing, the picnic they were having that

Friday. I'm glad I did because in my sophomore year I had learned to manage my time so much better and now I go to like half of the stuff—but if I had just walked out at first, I'd never have met these guys and they are my main friend group.

—Todd

Every club asks its members to be involved to some degree. It might not be a formal requirement, but there is an expectation that if you are a member of a group you contribute in some way. This might be as little as attending the general membership meetings or the club may ask you to attend a certain number of group events during the year.

You can check out any club by attending a meeting, you are not committing to it by just attending. You can ask others that are part of the group how often the group meets, what type of activities they have, how much time people generally put into the group, and how they like it. Make sure you get more than one opinion! Once you have a sense of how much time it takes, then you can decide if it fits in your schedule. You want to have enough time to put into the group to get the benefits of being involved, while ensuring that it does not require more time than you are willing or able to give. The amount of time you have available might also dictate how many groups you get involved with.

6.4: Types of Clubs and Organizations

As indicated earlier in this chapter, not every school has the same clubs, but there are some general categories that a club or organization might fall into. Below is a listing of those groupings and some of the types of clubs that you might find.

Academic. Academic clubs can include honor societies and clubs that focus on specific majors or careers. These clubs often offer opportunities for mentoring from faculty and/or working professionals, networking opportunities, and special events such as trips and speakers.

While faculty may often advise clubs, their level of involvement often varies by club and/or college. With academic clubs however faculty tend to be more involved, so this can often provide opportunities to get to know faculty outside of class.

Social planning.   Social planning will often be a part of many clubs, so you could also help with social planning as part of a club or organization. There is usually a group on campus that is responsible for activities on campus for all students. These groups are often advised through the student activities office and can be a part of student government, can be elected positions, or can be open to anyone interested. They often get their funding from student activities fees and decide what kinds of films, concerts, and other activities to plan for the whole campus.

VOICES FROM CAMPUS 6.2

Brandy

I was on the campus activities board and we plan spring fling. My senior year we had one of my favorite bands, and I got to meet the band and sit backstage for their rehearsal. The lead singer signed my hat and it was just completely mind blowing.

—Brandy

Arts, theater, dance, vocal, instruments.   This is a big category that encompasses many types of activities. At bigger schools or schools with majors in these areas there can be competition to be involved in some of these activities. Even if some of them are competitive clubs, you can often find less-competitive or non-competitive clubs as well. If you want to be in a play but don't get selected in tryouts, you can still be involved in lots of other ways. You can help with promotion, set design or building, ushering, and more. As with other clubs, getting involved in the beginning of your time will help you get more and more responsibility as you continue to be involved each year.

Sports clubs. Club sports will be covered in the next chapter.

Journalism and media. TV, radio, newspaper, and film have some of the same competitive components as the arts groups above. The bigger the school, the more difficult it may be to have significant responsibility in some of these groups—it will depend on who runs the group, how it is funded (the academic department or the student activities office), and the skill level of those involved. If you find it hard to break in, don't get discouraged, keep trying.

Political. While political groups are most often college democrats and republicans, some campuses also have libertarian, green party, or other groups. Some may be nonpartisan and work on getting out the vote or may be issue specific such as environmental policies, immigration concerns, etc. During election years these groups may be particularly visible and provide a great way to get involved in both local and national politics. They often will have connections in the community and can help you understand and get experience in how to engage in the political process.

Identity based. College is a time when you are figuring out who you are and who you want to be. You will come into contact with people who have different backgrounds, values, and cultures. This is an exciting time, but it can also be exhausting. Learning from and about others that are different than you is a part of life, but students who find themselves in the minority at their college can at times feel isolated, misunderstood, or get tired of explaining themselves to others. Or this might be the first time you realize you identify as a different gender than you were assigned at birth, start to acknowledge or explore feelings of attraction to different genders, or start thinking more about your race, culture, income level, abilities, religion, or age. Students in the minority on a campus will often form groups to help explore who they are within a group of similar people in order to feel safe and accepted. Some of these safe spaces are official offices on campus such as the women's center, the LGBT center, and the multicultural office. These offices often have student groups that meet and plan activities for their identity group. Even if there is not an office on campus for your specific identity group, there are often groups that meet around identity groups.

VOICES FROM CAMPUS 6.3

Sam

I came from a fairly conservative area and while I knew I was gay when I was in middle school, I didn't tell anyone. When I went to college I thought, okay, now I'll tell people. But when I got there, I didn't know where to start or how to do it. I saw there was a gay group on campus and I was afraid to go to the meetings because I was like, then people will know I'm gay! But then I realized that is kind of what I wanted, but I didn't know how to talk about it. I went to the alliance group meeting and everyone was supportive and caring and they didn't force me to do anything I didn't want to do. I was so afraid they'd make me come out right away or pressure me into only hanging out with gay people. But instead I found friends who supported me as I tried to figure it out. I'm involved in a lot of things on campus, but the alliance group is where I really found a home.

—Sam

Student government. Student government is a part of almost all campuses, but it can look different depending on the school. Most often there is a main student government with representatives elected during the spring. They will also often have a fall election for first-year representatives. There may also be volunteer positions and appointed positions. Student government's role on campus is very dependent on the campus culture. Student government elections can be a combination of high school dynamics of popularity and real world politics of who you know, the time you put in, and your platform.

At some colleges student government has a lot of power—students on these campuses feel like they have a voice. At these colleges the student government will often have some access to the president, may have a seat on the board of trustees, and will be involved in making recommendations to the college administration. If you are looking for a school where the students are listened to, looking at the student government will tell you a lot. If you want to be on student government and have a voice, then you should ask questions on your admissions tours or contact the student government president and ask about who they get to meet with and what changes they have been able to make. If they cannot list important committees or people at the college or they cannot name anything they have be able to do to make changes for students, then there is a good chance that the student government is more like the second type described below. This is not good or bad, it is just good to know as you consider what is important to you about how the school is run and what your experience might look like.

On other colleges student government serves as more of a programming board and they have minimal input on campus policies and governing. They get feedback from students and pass it along, but they are not in meetings where decisions are made and they tend to focus on planning social events.

On bigger campuses student government positions can be paid and they will sometimes also have the opportunity to go to regional or national student government conferences.

Residence hall government. Another form of student government that exists on campuses with residence halls is hall government. It is often called hall council, house council, or residence hall association. Sometimes the officers of the residence hall council serve on a council for all residence halls and even have a seat at student government. These councils serve to advise the residence hall director about concerns in the residence hall, look to create community through programming, and on some campuses will work to solve problems within a residence hall. Because their responsibilities are more "local" to their hall, it can feel more like you have an impact than student government that is working to make campus-wide changes. However your power and influence is limited to the residence hall and there is often a great deal of turnover from year to year as students change halls. This is a great way to meet people in the hall and to plan fun programs. Some schools are also connected with larger regional and national organizations for residence hall governments and there can be opportunities to go to a conference if you are involved in your residence hall.

Faith-based. Churches in the area are always glad to have college students attend, but they do not always have programs or groups in place to address student needs. The bigger the campus and the closer a church is to campus, the more likely they will have specific outreach or programs for college students. Campuses will often have a campus minister and/or a campus ministry office who is nondenominational and works to provide advice, guidance, and programming for a wide range of faiths. Sometimes local clergy will volunteer on campus in place of campus ministry.

Student groups are often connected to these offices or local churches or chapters of national groups such as fellowship of Christian athletes, Neumann centers, Hillel, Intervarsity, Muslim student organization, and many more (this is not meant to promote any of these above others or endorse them, it is just a sampling of some common groups). Campus ministry groups will often do volunteer work, have retreats, and share common practices of the faith.

Fraternities and sororities. Fraternities and sororities are some of the oldest student organizations on college campuses. Most likely you have an impression of them based on TV, movies, social media, or friends. These impressions are based on stereotypes and do not represent the wide range of fraternities and sororities that exist on campuses today. We will discuss a few of the basics you should know about the different types of organizations. We will provide a broad understanding of the variety of over 100 groups in the country and dispel some myths and misconceptions. So to start, let's talk about what is true and is not true.

YOUR TURN 6.3

Impressions of Fraternities and Sororities

A fraternity's main function is to have large social parties with alcohol	T	F
You have to live in the house in order to be a member	T	F
All fraternities haze their pledges	T	F
Being in a sorority is basically paying for friends	T	F
All fraternities and sororities are mostly white	T	F
All fraternities are all men and all sororities are all women	T	F
All fraternities and sororities have a national organization	T	F

This quiz is asking you about your knowledge of these organizations based on some of the more prominent stereotypes of fraternities and sororities. Because they are some of oldest organizations on campus and also many have national organizations that help promote them, they tend to get a lot of attention—and anything they do that is negative gets reported in the news. This doesn't mean they are all bad. In fact, the more positive aspects of them do not always get reported or mentioned. Before we talk about the quiz answers, there are a few terms that will help make sense of this section. Fraternities and sororities are often called Greeks as a shorter way to refer to them. When they are recruiting new members they have a time of the semester when they host social events, this is called rush. After rush is over you get a "bid," which is an invitation to join. If you say yes to joining, you go through a period of training where you learn about the organization and do activities to get to know the others members (new members are called pledges). This time period is called pledging or pledge period. At the end of pledging, you are initiated (or accepted fully as a member). So now that you know that, let's go over that quiz. If you haven't guessed by now, all the answers are false. Let's talk about why.

Q. A fraternity's main function is to have large social parties with alcohol

A. Greeks have a number of goals including service, leadership, brother-hood/sisterhood, and academics. Many Greeks do have social events, and in some organizations, some of these events are centered around alcohol. Every Greek has a different reputation on campus. These reputations are usually based on their actions on campus, so reputations should not be ignored. In addition to hearing others' impressions of the group, you should go check out the group yourself to see what they are like. Doing this before rush week (where you go to social events specifically to see which ones you might be interested in joining) is especially important as you will have a more realistic sense of the organization if you go when they are not trying to convince you to join. If you listen to what the members talk about, how their parties are advertised, who attends, the behavior of the members at parties, how they treat men and women, and their attitude about alcohol, grades, and college you should get an idea of what they are like and whether their goals and values match your own.

Q. You have to live in the house in order to be a member

A. Not every Greek even has a house, so this statement is false. However on some campuses some groups may require you to live in the chapter house for a period of time. In addition to the official houses, on bigger campuses they might have official houses and unofficial houses. Why does this matter? Well the role of the house in the organization and your require-ments if you join are important to consider. If they do have a house, they will sometimes require new members to live in it. If that is the case and you decide to pledge, then you want to know that information before you decide to pledge. Some people love living in a house with other students, others find it hard to study with so many people around. Additionally if you live there you are often also required to do some part of the cleaning, planning social events, and other things. Some houses have dining included and others do not. Your financial aid might also be covering housing but might not cover Greek housing. Some additional things to ask about Greek housing:

Is the house college owned, nationally owned, or private? Every campus is different and every group is different. On some campuses you can find all three of these situations.

1. If the college owns and runs it, you may be required to leave housing over breaks, may have college staff living in the house, and you may pay for housing directly to the college. The college will take care of maintenance in the house, but usually not cleaning. If the college owns the house, then you will have the same policies as residence halls, but you will also have more legal and financial protection.

2. Other times the national organization or the alumni of the group own the house and rent it to the group. This arrangement will often allow you to stay in the house year round. And you may find that the responses to problems or issues are better than they would be with a landlord. However, that is not always the case, so you'll want to ask about how maintenance issues are handled when they arise. This might not seem like a big deal to you as you read this, but if the heat breaks or there is a leak and you can't get anyone to come deal with it, it will feel very important at that point. This question applies to all types of ownership, but it can be harder to get a response when the house is not owned by the college. If the college owns the house, you can always call the head of Greek life for help.

3. If a group of members lease it, it is actually not associated with the fraternity even if people call it by the group's name or letters. This

means it would be the same as leasing a house off campus. Groups will sometimes have unofficial houses to avoid being caught by the college having parties. If your name or your parents are on the lease, you could be held liable for anything that happens in the house including damages, violation of local alcohol laws, and liability.

If you are considering living in a house, you should ask about the ownership situation. Also consider asking about who cleans the house, whether there are other fees associated with cleaning and/or dining, and whose names are on the lease and how that is handled. It's also important to ask if it's the official or unofficial house. Unofficial houses are often ways the groups get around the social hosting policy of the university and are more likely to be in places were large unregulated parties are thrown. If you live in an unofficial house, you can expect a lot of activity, a lot of mess, and the police showing up at your house at some point.

Q. All fraternities haze their pledges

A. What is hazing? According to Hazingprevention.org, "Hazing is any action taken or any situation created intentionally that causes embarrassment, harassment, or ridicule and risks emotional and/or physical harm to members of a group or team, whether new or not, regardless of the person's willingness to participate."

Every campus has hazing policies and most states have laws against hazing. However that does not mean that fraternities do not do some type of hazing. This is actually true in any organization, not just Greeks; however, Greeks have historically participated in hazing. Since it is illegal to haze, current members will often tell you they do not do it or will downplay what they do. This is where asking around campus about the reputation of the group can be very helpful. Some groups do minimal pledging activities that involve minor hazing such as wearing the same clothes or having to walk across campus in a line in a certain way, while other groups do much more extreme things like making you sleep in the basement for days without bedding, asking you to drop everything at any hour of the day or night and running to help another member, or drinking excessive amounts of alcohol. No hazing is okay, but only you can decide what membership is worth to you. You should go in knowing exactly what you are willing and not willing to do and also be familiar with your college's hazing policy and how to get help if you find yourself in over your head.

Q. Being in a sorority is basically paying for friends

A. For some reason this often gets said more about sororities than fraternities, but what it is referencing is that most Greeks have membership dues. These can range from minimal expenses to very pricey. These dues pay for social activities as well as membership to national organizations. Because Greek membership is fairly formal and connected to greater resources than your chapter, this helps maintain the organization and all the functions associated with it. If you are deciding to join a group, you should ask about the membership dues so you know what you'll be committing to.

Q. All fraternities and sororities are mostly white

A. Historically colleges began at a time when minorities did not have full citizenship rights and therefore these organizations were all white. As with many organizations across the country, some are now more integrated than others. Given the historical membership discrimination, some minority groups have chosen to create their own organizations that focus on similar goals of traditional Greeks but are also about empowering and equipping people from their identity group. There are Black Greeks, Latino Greeks, Asian Greeks, Jewish Greeks, and Gay Greeks. If your college does not have a Greek organization for your identity group, you can often affiliate with a chapter at another college in the area who does. If this is something you're interested in, spend some time searching online and contacting the national organization of the group that interests you.

Q. All fraternities are all men and all sororities are all women

A. While many are still single sex, there are co-ed Greeks. They used to be the service Greeks, but some campuses are requiring Greeks to go co-ed.

Q. All fraternities and sororities have a national organization

A. Most Greeks do have a national organization that you are joining when you join the group on your campus (called the chapter). If they are not affiliated with a national organization, they are called local—meaning that students at the college started the group at some point. Local groups do not have the same level of training and insurance as those associated with national groups, and they also do not have the benefits of networking and support that national groups can provide. Joining a local Greek group is more like joining a club or organization than joining a Greek group.

Pros and Cons of Joining a Greek Organization

Greek organizations can be a bit more intense than other organizations. Unlike other groups, once you join you are expected to remain a member and be involved in certain ways. If you want to quit, you have to "deactivate" and let the organization know you are no longer interested in being in the group. Given this level of commitment, joining a Greek group should not be done without a bit of thought and research. Your family, peers, and college will all have ideas about whether joining a Greek group is good or not, but only you can decide if it's right for you. Here are a few potential pros and cons of joining that you might consider.

Pros:

- If you are joining a national organization, you are connected through a common membership and experience to a national (or international) group of people. They will help you during and after college with internships, networking, and other opportunities.

- Some Greek chapters are very large and you will have a built-in group of people to hang out with and get to know while in college. It can provide a very structured way to get to know people and make friends.

- There are many opportunities for leadership within Greek organizations.

- Greeks are often involved in community service and so you will have opportunities (and expectations) to help with community service.

- On many campuses students in Greek organizations have better overall GPAs than their non-Greek peers. During pledging, GPAs will often get lower. However, during their overall college career, Greeks on average have higher GPAs than their non-Greek peers.

Cons:

- It can be costly. Between membership dues and other activities, the cost of Greek life can add up quickly.

- Due to high profile cases nationally where Greeks have hazed others or died from overdosing on alcohol, there can be a negative stigma attached to being a part of Greek life either on campus or when you job search.

- Some, not all, Greeks do haze and do have social scenes where drinking alcohol is expected and attitudes towards women are demeaning.

Other Special Interests

The list above is not exhaustive. There are many other types of clubs or organizations on campus including entrepreneurs, language clubs, solar race teams, outdoors or hiking clubs, and more. The bigger the school, the more clubs and organizations they have.

Student Leadership Opportunities

As we discussed earlier in this chapter, getting involved in a club or organization can lead to leadership opportunities in those clubs. There are often other opportunities on campus for student leadership through leadership programs. Students often find out about these opportunities through their clubs. But if you are interested to know if there is a program to learn more about leadership, your student affairs office is a good place to ask.

You Can Start Your Own

If after all this you still have not found a club or organization that meets your needs, you can often start your own. Every campus is different, but you can ask in the student activities office if this is possible and, if so, how to do it. It takes a lot of organization and determination; so before you head down this path, make sure you are really committed to doing this and that there is a group of people on campus who are also interested. You'll need more than just you to start a club.

6.5: The Take Away

- Before you decide what to get involved in, make sure to take the time to think about what you want. Don't just jump in or do what all your friends are doing.

- Make sure you go to the activities fair during orientation or the first few weeks of school.

- Consider your goals, the time you want to spend, and your interests as you decide what to join.

- Try something new—college is a time to explore.

- Trying something out is not a commitment; you can decide you don't like a group you joined.

- There is something for everyone.

PLAYING A SPORT IN COLLEGE

THERE'S MORE THAN JUST VARSITY

I loved playing football. I knew I wasn't good enough to play at a big school, but I wanted to go to one. So I thought I had to pick either Division III to play or Division I to have a great football school. Either I could play or not. I ended up at a Division I school, but then I found the sprint football club. I get to play football for fun and also attend a school with a big-time football team.

—Mike (Freshman year)

When you think of college sports you probably think of March madness or bowl games. But if you've ever played a sport and like doing so, there are opportunities to play that sport in college that don't involve Division I sports. There are three different ways that sports are organized at college.

1. The first type of sports at college are the ones you are most familiar with. These are what you called varsity sports in high school. They are organized by the school and have formal leagues, coaches employed by the school, uniforms, etc. There are different levels of varsity sports at colleges called divisions. These are regulated by the National Collegiate Athletic Association (NCAA) or the national Association of Intercollegiate Athletics (NAIA).

2. The second type of sports at college are called club sports. These are organized by students. They are not part of the NCAA and do not have formal leagues that are regulated and governed by the college. They will often play other schools that also have club teams. They are most often coached by students but they can sometimes have a part-time paid coach. They are funded by players and/or the student activities fees.

3. Finally there are intramurals. These are organized by the athletic department and have leagues where students play other students at the college, are refereed by other students, and have certain sports at certain times of the year.

There are also many pick-up games that will happen, and occasionally there are sporting events between residence hall groups, Greek life groups, and groups of friends. I'll leave it up to you to find those when you're at school.

Before you dive into reading about each type, take a minute to think about what is most important to you in playing a sport at college.

YOUR TURN 7.1

Why play a sport?

Rank what's most important to you in playing sports at college with 1 being most important and 10 being least important. At the end of the chapter we will note which choices align with which type of organization (1, 2, or 3 above).

_____ Playing time

_____ Getting a scholarship

_____ Having time to do things other than my sport

_____ Supportive teammates versus fierce competition for spots

_____ Flexibility to go to practices

_____ The chance to travel as part of the sport

_____ Having all expenses paid for my sport

_____ Focus on fun versus winning

_____ Chance to play something I'm interested in versus good at

_____ Chance to play more than one sport

Deciding whether to play sports during college will depend on your interest, your skill level, and your time commitment. If you are a great athlete you are probably already aware of your options. You may have already been contacted by recruiters or sent a video of yourself playing to some colleges. If you are being contacted by a recruiter it can be easy to get caught up in the hype and thrill of being wanted. You are also most likely aware of the various divisions, whether they offer scholarships, and how competitive the school is in your sport. Before making a decision about attending a college to play varsity sports, it is important to consider the time commitment, the financial commitment, and the other things you want to do in college.

Division I athletics are the most competitive and most time consuming of all college sports. Generally Division I athletes have little time to do anything else in season, and oftentimes there are off-season requirements that include training, lifting, and doing other activities that will improve performance. Division II also offers scholarships. Division III does not offer scholarships, but often coaches can get additional grants or loans for college athletes. While most people believe that getting a full ride to college based on athletics is common, in reality those scholarships go to the top athletes who are most likely going to go pro. Getting a partial scholarship or additional financial aid is a much more likely scenario for most high school athletes looking to play sports in college.

If you visit a college or get a call from a coach and are thinking about being on a team, there are some important questions to ask as you consider your options.

1. **Frequency and length of practices in season.**

    Practice for the fall season starts before school starts, so you will have to return to school earlier than other students, often in early to mid-August. You can check out each sport and their official practice and playing times here http://www.ncaa.org/playing-rules/playing-and-practice-season-charts. Pre-season practices are often all day or are longer than in-season practices. Some sports practice twice a day, some practice every day, and some have field time plus film time. Asking how often you practice and for how long will give you an idea of the time commitment required outside of game time.

There are often expectations outside of practice as well including lifting or conditioning.

2. Requirements for off season, both formal and informal practices.

The NCAA has regulations for how much the team is allowed to make you practice off season. But just because you may not be officially allowed to practice, there may be expectations that you practice, strengthen, or condition off season. Even if the coach cannot make an official policy, the team will know what the coach expects and tell you. The coach will also know if you do what is expected and will use this information to make decisions about who gets to play.

3. Travel time to games and tournaments.

How far away are all the teams in the league? Does the team travel by van, bus, or plane? Do you have double headers (softball and baseball) when you travel? How many classes will you miss or are most games, meets, etc. on the weekends? Will you be expected to travel to tournaments over breaks? How long are you gone for games (travel time includes getting there in time to warm up, stopping for a meal on the way home, and sometimes overnight stays)?

4. What academic support is available?

The NCAA has guidelines about academic support and many schools require athletes to attend study halls. These are dedicated times where you must be present and "study." Some schools do a good job making sure you get time to study during these times, other times it is goof-off time and takes away from time you could actually study. Some schools also offer academic tutors for athletes.

The NCAA has rules about student athlete's grades. If you fall below a certain GPA, you will be unable to play. Asking about the team's GPA and majors can tell you a lot about the coaches and players commitments to their academics.

5. **Scholarship rules and regulations.**

If you get a scholarship is it guaranteed for four years? How are awards determined? Will you be asked to red-shirt for a year? Will you get the scholarship even if you are injured? If you are Division III how will aid be determined each year?

6. **How playing time is determined.**

Do they allow walk-ons? Are positions done purely by tryouts every year or is there some seniority? How is performance measured? How many people are they recruiting for your position?

7. **Regulations on your social life.**

In-season coaches usually have strict rules regarding your social time including curfew, alcohol use, and more. If you get in trouble on campus, there can be repercussions from the coach including not playing or losing a scholarship. Usually in the off season the coach is not as strict, but it doesn't hurt to ask. Coaches will also often have policies about how you can use social media both on and off season.

8. **What support is there for other college experiences like study abroad?**

Experiences in college can include many things such as study abroad, community service, and research. Will you be allowed to participate in any of these or are you expected to make this sport your priority at all times and not participate in other college experiences?

While the coach should be able to answer questions you have about any of the above, it can help to ask a current team member. Additionally if you can talk to someone who quit the team, you might get to see another perspective. There are no right or wrong answers to any of these questions, but you should ask them to see if varsity sports are right for you and to help you determine which school and sports program might be the best fit.

7.1: Club Sports

Clarence

Being from the north, many high schools had a hockey team or at least the town did. I was on the high school team and I was excited to play in college. But when I started looking at colleges I realized that many of the schools I wanted to go to didn't have varsity ice hockey. I was bummed out until a friend of mine told me he played on his college club ice hockey team. I didn't know there was such a thing, so when I looked at colleges I started looking at their club teams, not just their varsity teams. It opened up a lot more options.

—Clarence

Club sports are often organized by students looking for sports opportunities on campus other than those formally offered by the athletic department. Club sports are often sports that are regionally not as popular or more niche sports. Much like other clubs, students run club sports and they can be funded through the student activities fees. There are often additional costs students pay for club sports to help cover travel expenses, referees, uniforms, or field/rink rental. If the college has fields they can usually use those for free, but they have to plan around the varsity team's use.

Club teams will travel to other colleges who also have teams. These are not in leagues that match the league the school is in, but are based on who else has a team. The popularity of the club sport will generally determine how far and/or how many games a club team can have.

Since club teams are run by students, often they will elect a coach or rotate the coach. Some teams hire a part-time coach or an alumni will help out. Depending on who's running it, how long it has been around, and how competitive they are you may have a little more flexibility with club sports practices as they tend to be a bit more informal.

7.2: Intramural Sports

The college's recreation department usually runs intramural sports. You can find out more about intramural sports at your college through the recreation department or center. Intramural sports usually have "seasons" when they will post information about how you can get a team together. You will play other teams from your same college. Some colleges also offer recreation tournaments, especially for individual sports like racquetball and tennis.

The intramural teams have a wide variety of options that range from co-ed to single-sex teams in all different kinds of sports. One of the nice things about these is that they're free or fairly inexpensive. At times there might be a fee to join the team. That fee pays for the referee but also ensures that you show up since the school may be paying for referees, field or gym time, and someone to organize the schedule of events.

VOICES FROM CAMPUS 7.2

Adriana

I was always a great athlete. My dad used to tell me I could compete with the boys. I wanted to be on the boys' basketball team, but I wasn't allowed. I didn't really want to play college ball because I had other things I wanted to do. Then when I got to college I realized I missed it. Someone in my math class said they were getting an intramural basketball team together and they needed at least four girls for the team. He wanted to know if I was interested. I jumped at the chance even though he was only asking because they needed more girls for the co-ed league. Now we joke about it because I'm one of the best players! Anyway, I love playing but I can also miss a practice or a game if I need to for schoolwork, so it works out—except they don't like me missing games because they end up losing without me.

—Adriana

Intramurals often have prizes for winning the championship. These range from T-shirts to bragging rights to small monetary awards.

As with any sport, you will also have a range of competitiveness. Some leagues may be more competitive than others; some people may be more competitive than others. The great thing about intramurals is they are a great way to have fun, they last a short period of time, and they have little practice with maximum playing time. The downside is you can get on a team that doesn't show up or has an overly competitive person or two who ruin it for everyone (or perhaps you are very competitive and you think the non-competitive people ruin it for everyone). Some schools even advertise the level of competitiveness to help people understand what's expected of them so people can be in leagues that best match their interests. If you go in for the social aspects, the fun, and the exercise, you will find intramurals a great way to be a part of sports in college. If you are highly competitive, make sure you find teammates who are as well. Also understand that the referees are volunteer or paid student workers, so they are doing their best, but the level of officiating will not be the same as if you played varsity sports in high school. For the highly competitive player, keeping that in mind will keep you and your team from having unrealistic expectations of the officiating. If you want to earn a bit of extra money or you are sidelined due to an injury, recreation departments are often looking for refs.

If you get asked to be on a team, or you start one, make sure you ask about the expectations for practice time and who will be in charge of calling practices, collecting money, and deciding who plays and how much. If you're the organizer, you want to set the expectations about how competitive the team will be, how much practice will be required, and what expectations there are for attendance and games.

7.3: Your Turn Revisited

As you read through this chapter you probably were able to identify which type of organized sport matched your ranked choices in Your Turn 7.1, but here's a re-cap. The numbers correspond to the types at the beginning of the chapter: 1 = Varsity, 2 = Club, and 3 = Intramural.

Playing Time

1. You have very little control over this. This will be up to the coach, your ability, and your competition. You can be a starter one year and then a new recruit could beat you out.

2. You have some control. Club sports are focused on winning and the team will either have a coach or elect a player to coach. However, most club teams try to make sure everyone gets a chance to play.

3. Like #2, this might depend on how focused your team is on winning and how good you are. Some intramural leagues and/or teams are just for fun and everyone gets an equal chance. Others are very competitive and you may only be able to get a lot of playing time if you are good.

Getting a Scholarship

1. Scholarships are limited, but available for Division I and II. For Division III they are given out through financial aid packages.
2. None.
3. None.

Having Time to Do Things Other Than My Sport

1. In-season, varsity athletes have little time to do anything but practice, play, and go to class. Off-season Division II and III can offer more free time, but it will depend on the coach.
2. Club sports have a season and often just have pick-up games for fun or social time off season.
3. The only time commitments are during the "season."

Supportive Teammates Versus Fierce Competition for Spots

Do you have to try out for a position? Do you have to prove your worth every game or every season? Does the team get on your back if you mess up or are they encouraging no matter what? This isn't about the organizational type, it's about the culture of the team.

Flexibility to Go to Practices

1. You have to be at every practice. No excuses. Even if you are injured, you go and observe.
2. You should be at every practice, but if something major comes up the club is usually forgiving. They might have policies indicating that if you miss practice you can't play in the next game, but they generally have some flexibility.
3. Your team may or may not practice.

The Chance to Travel as Part of the Sport

1. You will travel to many games within your league and often travel to tournaments during breaks. Travel will be on college-owned or rented vehicles.
2. You will travel to other colleges to play. Sometimes you can borrow a school vehicle, but often you will have to rent a van or carpool.
3. You play on campus. You only travel to the gym or the field where you are playing.

Having All Expenses Paid for My Sport

1. If you are playing a varsity sport generally everything is paid for. Sometimes teams want to travel to tournaments that are not within the athletics budget, especially at Division III schools, and team members will do fundraisers to go.

2. The college does not fund club sports except for what comes out of the student activities fee. They are funded like any other club. Depending on how much they get and also what the team wants—a part-time coach, cool uniforms, league and referee fees, tournament fees, and travel—they will also do fundraisers to help pay the cost of these expenses.

3. Intramurals usually have a small entry fee to pay for referees. Sometimes you get a portion back if you show up for all your games but lose it if you forfeit it. Teams will also sometimes pitch in for matching shirts. They do not do fundraising, but ask each member to help by paying a small amount.

Focus on Fun Versus Winning

Some people do not see these as different things—they only have fun if they win. But in general, getting a good idea of how important winning is to you will matter no matter which choice you make, and that will depend on the coach, the team, and your teammates. While intramural leagues sometimes have different "divisions" to note how competitive they are, sometimes they do not. If you don't like a highly competitive atmosphere, you should speak to the coach and other players to get an idea of how intense the team is.

Chance to Play Something I'm Interested in Versus Good At

1. Obviously you have to be good.

2. Depending on the school and the interest level you may be able to play on a team where you are not great and learn to get better. Even if you can't play in games, you might be able to practice with the team.

3. As long as you can get a team together or find one to play on, you can enter any league you want.

Chance to Play More Than One Sport

1. At Division I you generally only play one sport. In some Division II or III schools you could be in more than one sport in different seasons.

2. You can play on as many club teams as you have time for, but most likely one per season.

3. You can play on as many intramural teams as you have time for. You can even play on more than one sport at a time.

7.4: The Take Away

- There are a variety of options when it comes to playing sports in college.

- If you are recruited for a team, make sure to do your homework before committing.

- Sports can be a great way to get involved, meet people, and have a great college experience. You just have to decide how much time you want to spend playing sports versus doing other things and then make your choices accordingly.

A WORD ABOUT FACULTY AND STAFF

My work-study was in the English department filing things. Honestly it was pretty boring, but I got to do some homework when we were not busy. Over my first year I got to know a professor who was writing a book that sounded interesting. The more I talked to her the more interested I got in the book. One day she asked me if I wanted to be part of the team doing research for the book. I didn't really know what that meant but I thought why not? What started as me asking some questions turned out to be a year-long project and I even got mentioned in a published book.

—Xiang (Senior year)

I n this book we talk a lot about how important it is to get involved and then we talk about a variety of ways you can get involved at college. This idea—that being involved matters for your college experience—is based on many studies looking at who succeeds in college and why. We know that students who get involved do better. You might assume that this is because having friends at college will make it more enjoyable and you will be more likely to stay. This is true. But we also know that students who interact with faculty outside of class are more likely to have good grades and more likely to graduate. But what does it mean to interact with faculty "outside of class" and how do you do that?

A few of the things we discussed in this book could lead to interacting with faculty outside of class, including joining an academic club or doing work-study in an academic office. You will get a lot of help and advice and how to succeed academically in high school, college orientation and from various people at college. This advice may include (as it should) getting to know your faculty - but it can be difficult to know how to interact with faculty outside of class. Of course you can—and should—go to faculty office hours, but there is more to it than that.

Aside from faculty there are administrators and staff who you will also get to know in college. These are your advisors, career counselors, residence hall directors, club advisors, coaches, and more. These people are all there to make sure your college experience is the best it can be and they work to make sure you have not only a safe college experience but that your time outside of the classroom is equally beneficial.

Before we talk about how to get to know faculty, let's take a minute to think about the people during high school who were important to you or helped you to succeed.

YOUR TURN 8.1

All the Adults in Your High School and What
You Did or Can Learn From Them

List all the people in high school who helped you succeed. You can list peers and your parents, but this exercise is really focused on all the other people you might have interacted with (e.g., coaches, teachers, your youth pastor). If you do not have anyone, then think about your friends or peers and who you think helped them.

List people here:

_____

_____

_____

_____

For each of these people, identify how you got to know them:

_____

_____

_____

_____

Looking at the ways you got to know them, consider if it was from a formal activity like class, a sports team, or some other planned program or did you meet them some other way?

_____

_____

_____

_____

Finally, what did they do that helped you succeed?

_____

_____

_____

_____

Hopefully you were able to identify people who helped you along the way. My guess it that many of them you initially met because of some activity or class. You may have met them that way but at some point they encouraged you, talked to you, or did something to support you that mattered. The same thing will be true in college. You have to get involved in something in order for it to lead to a meaningful supportive or mentoring relationship. It doesn't happen magically.

So as you see from Your Turn 8.1 getting involved can lead to success. Hopefully at least one of the people you identified from your list was a teacher. Perhaps it was someone who inspired you in class, encouraged you to try harder or try again, or just made you feel like you could succeed. There are faculty like this in college as well. Getting to know them outside of class can really help you succeed. They often know people in your field either working or teaching at another school. They can help you network for a job. If you plan on going to graduate school, you will be required to have a letter of reference from faculty members.

VOICES FROM CAMPUS 8.1

Alex

After I realized I wanted to major in psychology I knew I had to get a master's degree. This was not at all my plan when I went to college, but I went to a program in the library where a faculty member was talking about a book she wrote and it was so interesting. I decided to take the class she taught and then I took another. I went to office hours to discuss her work and it was her idea that I might like psychology. I told her no way because I knew I would need a master's degree. But she helped me realize that doing what I love is important, so in the end that is what I did. She talked to me about different schools and in the end she not only wrote my letter of recommendation but through a connection helped me get an assistantship to help pay for grad school.

—Alex

8.1: Undergraduate Research

Aside from just getting to know faculty and asking them for help in office hours, there are two specific things that you can do with faculty that we know will lead to your success: undergraduate research and a senior thesis or capstone. Faculty members do research as a part of their job. If you go to the college's website and look up the faculty, you will see it lists their area of research. If you find something that is interesting to you, you should consider taking that faculty member's class. Additionally, you should ask that faculty member about their research. You should also ask your advisor and your faculty if there are opportunities to get involved in research. This means that you would be helping the faculty member with their research. It can range from going on an archeological dig, doing research for a book, helping run experiments in the lab, and so much more. Working side by side with faculty on applying academic knowledge to practice will help you understand class concepts, engage you in learning in a new and interesting way, and build important and lasting mentorship relationships with faculty.

8.2: Senior Thesis or Capstone

Some schools also offer (or require depending on the major) the opportunity to do a senior thesis or capstone. This is like the research done above, except that you pick the problem you want to study, work with a faculty member to come up with a project, and then learn how to research it. It can be a challenging experience, but it helps you draw on all the things you learned in college and do one large project at the end to bring it all together. These can last a semester or a year. If your college does not offer these options, you can also ask a faculty member if you can do an independent study with them. This means that the faculty member will work with you one on one to come up with what you want to learn and how you want to learn it. This might not sound like something you are interested in now as it's usually done during the junior or senior year of college, but you should be open to the idea of doing one of these two things. The more you attend lectures, programs, and events on campus that have an academic focus, the more likely you are to find something that really interests you—when you do, spending time researching it might sound very interesting.

8.3: The Take Away

- Faculty and staff on campus can be very important people to get to know.
- Working with faculty on projects outside of class leads to success.
- Take advantage of opportunities to learn about academic ideas outside of class as often as you can.

EXPLORING BEYOND CAMPUS

My sophomore year my environmental science class went to a local park and learned about their conservation program. The park was less than a mile from campus but I had never been there. I couldn't believe this cool thing was so close to me and I never knew.

– Brandi, Junior

Whether you are attending college where you live or you are going to college in another place, there is life beyond the college campus that can add to your college experience.

9.1: Being a Local at Your College

If you are going to a college near home, college is still a chance to see your town in a new light. As a kid you went to things your parents took you to and as a high school student you did things with your peers that were most likely the "regular hangouts." As a college student, you are learning a new way to see things—and you are now an adult—learning to live in a community on your own terms. You will be learning things in class that will offer new perspectives and you will be meeting people who are not from the area.

As a local you can be a tour guide and host to students who are not from the area. This will help with a new perspective. Hearing what others think and experience about your home will provide you will new and interesting insights. Try to find things to do that you have not done before or go to things you have seen before and consider how others in your community experience them differently than you do. Consider inviting international students home with you for the holidays. They can't go home and they would love a chance to be with a family over the holidays.

9.2: Going away to College

If you go away to college, do not get stuck in the "bubble" of your campus. This may be the only time in your life that you get to live in this town. Take advantage of your free time, your freedom and your own curiosity. There will be places that the students hang out, but do not limit yourself to just those places. Be a tourist in the town. You will not feel like you have time to do this, but once you have a full time job you will realize just how much free time you had and wish you had done more exploring.

Checking out the local (affordable) food scene is often what students are drawn to, but go beyond what is near college and find ethnic food places, food trucks or places the locals go. Use these outings to learn more about the community. By observing a town and the community you can reflect on what will be important to you when you decide where to live.

Use your College ID to your advantage

Many museums, movie theaters and cultural attractions want students to experience what they have to offer but also realize you may have limited funds. Check out things in your area that have reduced fees when you show your college ID. Make sure you take your college ID with you everywhere you go, especially if you travel abroad. My museums offer lower prices to college students. There are also many chain restaurant and stores that offer discounts with a college ID. Make sure you do an internet search on college ID discounts, you will be amazed at what you find.

YOUR TURN 9.1

How do I find out?

Ask adults in your life (parents, relatives, friends of your parents, youth pastor, etc.) how they find out about what is happening in their community. List what they say here.

_____

_____

_____

_____

Now go look at the sources they mentioned. What activities do you see that you did not know were happening in your own city or town?

_____

_____

_____

_____

Pick the city or town where one of the colleges you are interested in is located. Look for similar resources as the ones above and list them here.

_____

_____

_____

_____

Finally, pretend you are going to your town as a tourist and look up sites about what they recommend for activities in the area.

Finding Out About What is Happening

As a high school student you knew about what was happening from friends, from social media or your high school. You most likely did not think about events in the community beyond your circle of friends. There is a whole world of activity that happens in every town that many teenagers do not pay attention to or know about. These include art shows, theater shows, festivals, music, parks and other special events in the community. Search facebook, twitter and instagram for community events and organizations in the area and then follow or like them to get news about events. Even though you get most of your information on line, many places still publish local newspapers or magazines. They may be available on line as well, but not always. Go to the local coffee shops and read the bulletin boards or pick up a local paper. Search the internet for neighborhood organizations such as civic or community groups. Look up the local library (not your college library) and check out their events. Look on Yelp, Travelocity and other apps that people who travel to your town use when they are visiting. Finally, the faculty and staff you interact with live in this community full time and year round. Ask them what they do for fun and how they find out about activities.

VOICES FROM CAMPUS 9.1

Jared

For my history of jazz music class we had to go see a local jazz show. Everyone in class knew of this one place to go so we made a plan to go see a show there. In looking it up on line I found a group of local musicians that played at the same place on their open mic night. After listening to some samples of the music there was one artist I really liked. Then I saw he was playing at some coffee shop in town I had not been to. I decided to check it out and next thing I know I found this whole world of local music I didn't know about. I'm glad I stumbled onto it my sophomore year because I spent my last two years exploring the local music scene and I made all sorts of interesting friends and got to experience a part of the town I probably never would have seen.

—Jared

Impress Others in a Job Interview

Unless you get involved in the local community, you might not be able to put your exploration on your resume. But talking about how you went outside of "regular college student" activities when you are in a job interview will show your interviewer that you are curious, someone who thinks outside the box and is willing to take risks. You could also get to know people in the community by become involved or talking to people when you attend events. Through this networking you might find interesting and unusually connections that could lead to internships or jobs. Others like when people are interested in them and what better way to have a connection with someone than sharing a common interest. If you are a college student who is going off the beaten path, community members will appreciate that you went beyond the campus to get to know the local community.

9.3: The Take Away

- Whether you are going to college locally or in another place, exploring beyond campus will add to your college experience

- This may be the last time you live in this city or town, so take advantage of your free time

- Use local resources including people, groups and publications targeted towards the community to find out what is happening

BIBLIOGRAPHY

Astin, A. W., Vogelgesang, L. J., Ikeda, E. K., & Yee, J. A. (2000). How service learning affects students.

Astin, A. W. (1984). Student involvement: A developmental theory for higher education. *Journal of college student personnel*, *25*(4), 297–308.

Berger, J. B. (2000). Organizational behavior at colleges and student outcomes: A new perspective on college impact. *The Review of Higher Education*, *23*(2), 177–198.

Binder, J. F., Baguley, T., Crook, C., & Miller, F. (2015). The academic value of internships: Benefits across disciplines and student backgrounds. *Contemporary Educational Psychology*, *41*, 73–82.

Callanan, G., & Benzing, C. (2004). Assessing the role of internships in the career-oriented employment of graduating college students. *Education+ Training*, *46*(2), 82–89.

Cheng, D. X. (2004). Students' sense of campus community: What it means, and what to do about it. *NASPA journal*, *41*(2), 216–234.

Downs, P. E. (2003). Value of Recreational Sports on College Campuses-Introduction. *Recreational Sports Journal*, *27*(1), 5–8.

Dwyer, M. M., & Peters, C. K. (2004). The benefits of study abroad. *Transitions abroad*, *37*(5), 56–58.

Foubert, J. D., & Urbanski, L. A. (2006). Effects of involvement in clubs and organizations on the psychosocial development of first-year and senior college students. *NASPA journal*, *43*(1), 166–182.

Gilardi, S., & Guglielmetti, C. (2011). University life of non-traditional students: Engagement styles and impact on attrition. *The Journal of Higher Education*, *82*(1), 33–53.

Huang, Y. R., & Chang, S. M. (2004). Academic and cocurricular involvement: Their relationship and the best combinations for student growth. *Journal of College Student Development*, *45*(4), 391–406.

Kilgo, C. A., Sheets, J. K. E., & Pascarella, E. T. (2015). The link between high-impact practices and student learning: Some longitudinal evidence. *Higher Education*, *69*(4), 509–525.

Kuh, G. D. (2008). Excerpt from high-impact educational practices: What they are, who has access to them, and why they matter. *Association of American Colleges and Universities*.

Kuh, G. D., Kinzie, J., Schuh, J. H., & Whitt, E. J. (2011). *Student success in college: Creating conditions that matter*. John Wiley & Sons.

Kuh, G. D. (2009). What student affairs professionals need to know about student engagement. *Journal of college student development, 50*(6), 683–706.

McCluskey-Titus, P. (2003). Assessing What Students Learn from Involvement in Campus Activities. *Campus Activities Programming, 35*(7), 49–54.

McCormick, A. C., Moore, J. V., & Kuh, G. D. (2010). Working during college: Its relationship to student engagement and education outcomes. *LW Perna, Understanding the Working College Student*, 179–212.

Milem, J. F., & Berger, J. B. (1997). A modified model of college student persistence: Exploring the relationship between Astin's theory of involvement and Tinto's theory of student departure. *Journal of college student development, 38*(4), 387.

National Intramural-Recreational Sports Association (US) (Ed.). (2004). *The value of recreational sports in higher education*. Human Kinetics Publishers.

Paulsen, M. B. (Ed.). (2014). *Higher education: Handbook of theory and research* (Vol. 29). Springer.

Pike, G. R., & Askew, J. W. (1990). The Impact of Fraternity or Sorority Membership on Academic Involvement and Learning Outcomes. *NASPA journal, 28*(1), 13–19.

Seidman, A. (Ed.). (2005). *College student retention: Formula for student success*. Greenwood Publishing Group.

Skipper, T. L., & Argo, R. (Eds.). (2003). *Involvement in campus activities and the retention of first-year college students* (No. 36). National Resource Center for the.

Trowler, V. and Trowler, P. (2010) Student engagement evidence summary. York: Higher Education Academy

APPENDIX

WHERE TO TURN— ADDITIONAL RESOURCES

In Print

The Road to College: The High School Student's Guide to Discovering Your Passion, Getting Involved, and Getting Admitted (College Admissions Guides) Princeton Review; 1st edition, July 17, 2007

On the Web

North American Intrafraternity Conference
http://nicindy.org/

National Multicultural Greek Council (NMGC)
http://nationalmgc.org/

National Panhellenic Conference
https://www.npcwomen.org/about/member-organizations.aspx

The department of state information about study abroad
https://studyabroad.state.gov/

A clearing house for information about internships and internship opportunities
http://www.internshipprograms.com/

National Collage Athletic Association
http://www.ncaa.org/

Information about work study
https://studentaid.ed.gov/sa/types/work-study

Council on undergraduate research
http://www.cur.org/about_cur/

American student government association
http://www.asgaonline.com/ME2/Default.asp

National Association of College and University Residence Halls
http://www.nacurh.org/

Information about study abroad
https://www.studyabroad.com/

www.ingramcontent.com/pod-product-compliance
Lightning Source LLC
Chambersburg PA
CBHW071054280326
41928CB00050B/2509